ACKNOWLEDGEMENTS

Special thanks to Amanda Higginbotham and Shane Charania, as well as Nina Kamberos and Maxine Mills—generosity such as yours is a reminder that kindness runs this world far more often than we realize.

TRIPPING TO DICKEYLAND

IN MEMORIAM

James Dickey, 1923 – 1997

Chris Fuhrman, 1960 – 1991

and Jeanne Hudson, 1929 – 2010

TRIPPING TO DICKEYLAND

BY MICHAEL HANSON

EVERYTHING IS HOW MUCH GLORY IS IN IT . . . —JAMES DICKEY
. . . ONLY CONNECT . . . — E. M. FORSTER

Sinking again, like my life was rushing away from me and I couldn't cry or scream or say anything, only sit there with a scary cold emptiness closing itself around me while outside the window cardinals and robins and wrens were making the morning songs associated with my waking.

A friend had phoned first thing to tell me the news I naturally had no notion of, making it a rare exception to linger in bed on a Monday morning, and what could I say except thank you, thank you for calling to tell me what I never wanted to hear ever, that it was here finally and I'd have no choice but to face it, deal with it on this very day as well as every other one because now it would be the world I lived in, and what other luxury is one allowed in this life save that of living it? I slid suddenly down while hopes I had harbored for over a decade sank out of sight . . . again. What good does it do to prepare for these occasions when in fact we're never ready? I had anticipated this moment for so long that in a paranoid fit I was likely to think I willed it, caused it to occur by way of my worrying. And here it was on a cold morning in January, the calamity come to pass but the birds still singing in spite of it. With whom could I commiserate when the only one who would *really* get it (and who would have insisted we memorialize the moment in some symbolic fashion) had himself put me in these same sorry shoes six years prior, left me to live in a world without him in it? And here is where I found myself: hating the birds for their singing, hating my hopes and fantasies for not coming true, hating my life for being like all other ones. I had so wanted things to happen the way I envisioned them, and had committed myself to the task with the discipline of a drill instructor to see such things come to fruition. But boyhood dreams die hard, same as everything else.

I wish I could claim to have discovered poet/novelist James Dickey on my own, but naturally the credit goes to someone else— my friend Chris Fuhrman. I'd met Chris when I was eleven years old (he was fourteen): we'd both been cast in a Savannah Little Theatre production of a period comedy called *Life With Father*, and Chris was to play my older brother. Terrified, given that it was my first play and I knew none of the people in the cast, I'd hardly spoken to anyone when, one night during break, this older boy I'd just met said to me, 'Look here a minute.' Removing a single sheet of looseleaf paper from a spiralbound notebook, he began tearing it into squared sections, turning torn fragments he'd tear again and again while I wondered what in the world he was doing and why was I being asked to bear witness to it. When the sheet was at last reduced to what I imagined were dozens of small squares, he began to unfold it . . . opening the once-shredded but suddenly-restored sheet while my mouth dropped stupidly, astonished. And by the time he finished and handed me the creased but complete proof of this miracle and said, 'Take nothing for granted,' he was by then bored by it, walking away casually as if he'd already done for me all that he could.

Trust me—he'd do a lot more.

From my first memories of him, Chris was the one who stressed the importance of finding heroes—a point he proved to great effect by fast becoming the first hero this runty redhead ever met. Once, after I'd let slip a self-deprecating remark about being moody, to say nothing of *short*, he actually mailed me a letter. *You know what keeps me going?* he wrote. *Heroes. I'm not talking fictional bullshit, man, the toughest/coolest/highest achieving guys had* <u>*problems*</u>, *and MANY were short, under six feet definitely. Houdini, Faulkner, Hitchcock, I could keep going. You're a cool S-O-B, Hanson, and you'll make it* <u>*because*</u> *of your disadvantages. Isn't that some shit?* At the time I knew next to nothing about the names he'd mentioned, but I recognized them as famous, exceptional, and here was this guy I looked up to telling me I had something in common with them, something that connected me to them and could push me to rise above the ragged lot to reach the heights of dreams. It was like he could *see* something in me, something I'd not ever taken the time to look for.

Years would pass before James Dickey became a name of note for us, but once discovered he took a place of prominence because he was *alive*, and from Georgia, our home state. Chris had seen Dickey give a reading at a local college, was so blown-away by it that he immediately immersed himself, and a week later drove me to the now-defunct Colony Book Shop to purchase my own copy of a collection of poems by his newest hero.

First I was force-fed Dickey's enigmatic poem "The Sheep Child," whose subject of men coupling with sheep to produce the progeny of the title appealed to my 16-year-old sensibility by virtue of shock-value alone—Chris stood over my shoulder while I read it, saying over and over 'Can you believe it?' like he couldn't believe it himself. Like any dedicated pupil, I spent the next few days excitedly reading some of the less shocking ones on my own, and what struck me as a common element in all of what I read was the air of *silence*, the quiet way in which the poet worked his spell over you, even when the subject was something so obscene as a man having sex with a sheep.

Back then I wasn't as attuned to the man's image-making as I am now, but I knew right away that this poet had some kind of persuasive power over my emotions, even if I couldn't always articulate why or how. Chris, meanwhile, was taking his infatuation to the next level by learning everything he could about the creator, not limiting his knowledge to the work but including the life of the man who made it. And of course the more we learned the more fascinated we became. For us, James Dickey was like a living Ernest Hemingway, a literary force to be reckoned with, and not only did he embody the "man of action" persona that meant he lived life to the lees, he also was deadly serious about his art: the long, deliberate construction of a unique body of work that would seal for himself some semblance of immortality.

Which is to say that, along with getting some kind of work done with regard to writing, it also was imperative that one pursue the wild-to-be-wreckage approach to living that sometimes became the subject of literature. So when Chris read Dickey's "The Enemy From Eden," an essay about hunting rattlesnake with blowguns, it seemed not only natural but actually *necessary* that we get off our sleepy suburban asses and see for ourselves what such an endeavor entailed.

I thought he was just jiving us, but weeks later he called me to come over and there they were: they'd been delivered in a long cardboard box labeled HOUSE OF WEAPONS, three of them, each of which was six feet in length and equipped with twenty-five darts apiece. The weapon itself was essentially a hollow aluminum pipe splashed with army-green camouflage paint, to which one attached a swatch of foam-rubber (using similarly painted green tape they supplied) that served the same purpose as a quiver to a compound bow—into the spongy swatch one could easily poke six to ten darts, the rest required a carrying-case we ourselves fashioned from a small square of corrugated cardboard. We practiced only for a couple of weeks—firing the breath-propelled darts at an enlarged photocopy of a rattlesnake tacked to a big piece of found plywood—before deciding to do it for real by driving down into the bowels of some godforsaken outback of a place called Hortense, roughly two hours from home.

And what a day it turned out to be. Four of us crammed into the cab of a friend's pickup, we started the journey at five o'clock on a Saturday morning and didn't end it until nearly nine that night. I'll spare the reader the catalog of mishaps, for they were countless and exhausting and even a little disastrous, truth told, leading as they did to our hiking around in 95-degree heat all day, contaminating with gasoline one gopher hole after another in a futile attempt to find a rattler, then becoming mired in a muddy swamp with knee-deep water that suffocated the tires of our truck and from which it took us four-and-a-half hours to free ourselves . . . all of which resulted in our having spent nearly sixteen hours on a trip ("adventure," Chris would call it) that left us prematurely hungover (we'd killed two cases of beer), badly sunburned, and—icing on the shitcake—still snakeless. But now, years after the fact, my blowgun lazily stretched along a windowsill and covered by a thin film of undisturbed dust, the failure of our efforts to wrangle a rattler that day doesn't bother me in the least. Nor does the knowledge that my friends, only a month after our failed first attempt, actually went out again without me and on this occasion were successful, killing a rattlesnake over five feet long by way of nearly fifty blow-darts fired in succession. (I was, however, present for the ceremonial eating of said snake, cut into small bites and grilled in butter and garlic, the meat tough and rubbery and tasting nothing like chicken, as someone had said it would.) What matters most to my memory is that we did it: we went out and tried our hand at something completely different, albeit eccentric. And as Dickey had Lewis Medlock admonish us in the novel *Deliverance*, what counts in the end "is not going to be what your title says you do, but what you end up doing. You know: *doing*."

Dickey said the same of himself, of course: in the 1976 Paris Review Interview he confessed, "I'm the kind of person who can't be interested in a thing without wanting to see if I can't get out there and do a little of it myself." Chris and I thus inherited the same sense of wonder that Dickey seemed to embody, and we applied this approach not only to antics like blowgun-hunting but also to writing. Both of us had come to the decision to write completely independent of one another, even at different times in our life. I can't say for certain when it was that my friend made that resolution for himself, but for me it was the result of a gradual immersion into awareness that began right around the time I met Chris, yet sprung from a source that preceded him: Edgar Allan Poe. I'd plunged into Poe by way of a paperback mail-ordered from a middle-school catalogue: a book of short stories gratuitously given an ominous title, *Six Tales Of Terror* or some such nonsense, a successful strategy for coaxing youngsters to read the work of an artist who, come upon in a classroom literature text, would have been yet another of those subjects about which we would have remained entirely uninterested. But primed as any other 11-year-old for a tale of terror, I read that book with the relish of something longed-for, and found myself—if not terrified—completely captivated, mesmerized by the mysterious aura of stories like "The Tell-Tale Heart" and "The Fall Of The House Of Usher". To this very day I have a fondness for Poe that borders on reverence, for he managed to bridge the gap between what was fun to read and what was high art. And somewhat like the author I was later to learn so much from, I couldn't help but try my own inadequate hand at writing in the Poe vein. He had infected me with something, and even though I stopped after that initial burst, I began again years later, only this time around I approached it with the earnest sincerity of a dreamer, now believing the practice was a kind of addiction, and a *positive* one at that—a productive way to spend one's time in the world.

Buried in a box somewhere I still have two manila folders full of the stories and poems that were the product of my puerile, Poe-charged imagination, and while some might say that therein lies the beginning of my so-called literary efforts, for me that formidable occasion occurred when Chris and I made that trek to the Colony Book Shop to shell-out seven dollars for a book of poems by some guy named Dickey. In truth I wasn't really writing at this time, but the work in that book sparked something that caused me to begin *thinking* about writing, *serious* writing, and once I met the man himself whatever doubts kept me from diving head-on into the endeavor would be wiped-out, eliminated entirely.

I was a sophomore at the University of Georgia, and Chris (who'd barely graduated high school but was now an undergraduate at Yale) came south to stay with me for a couple of days because our main man of letters was to be part of a panel of writers the school was bringing to town for a celebration of area authors, even though of the five or six they brought not one of them still called the state their home. Once my friend arrived we hauled ourselves up into the north Georgia Appalachians to camp for a night in that section of the country Chris had taken to calling Dickeyland, since it was there the man had set his most famous book, but also because supposedly he still had relatives in the region. We rose early the morning following to head back to town, drinking the whole way in an effort to affect our hero's colossal appetite for alcohol, and also—I now suspect—to bolster our bravery, both knowing deep down that the day would be a waste were we unable to summon the simple but extraordinary courage required to shake his hand and say to him how strongly we felt about the work he was doing. Into the newly-built Student Center we dared to smuggle two sixteen-ounce cans of beer, which we cracked open audaciously in the middle of the crowd once we'd gotten in to where all the minions were mingling, awaiting the arrival of The Reader. When Dickey did appear, striding into the lobby outside the big open ballroom where the reading was to take place, he carried all of the larger-than-life charisma of a favorite movie star one was catching sight of for the very first time. He was an immense figure, over six feet with a barrel of a torso, wearing a black t-shirt beneath an open green blazer, a big medallion hanging halfway down his chest: it looked like some kind of creature skeleton encased in a clear, biscuit-thick plastic disk. On his head he sported an overlarge wide-brimmed hat with a diamond-patterned snakeskin wrapped around the rim. In truth he looked more like he had just come off a safari rather than was preparing to read poetry to a group of gawking academics at a university, where I got my first glimpse of the mystique Dickey had been building for himself over the thirty-year course of his career as a writer.

Which isn't to say it was an entirely false presentation, a lie Dickey fashioned and successfully perpetrated on the poetry-buying public. What Dickey's persona did was favor certain facets of his personality over other ones, which I'd later come to understand was his way of concealing the insecurities so few of us even knew he carried. He was without question an intellectual, having graduated *magna cum laude* from Vanderbilt, and maintaining ever since an encyclopedic knowledge of poetic tradition. But he tended to boast about other, less "literary" aspects of himself: that he liked to hunt with bow-and-arrow; had been a college athlete who played running back on the football team and ran high hurdles on the track team; not to mention was a war veteran (though not nearly so decorated as he'd led people to believe). In interviews he would excitedly recall archery tournaments he had won or canoe trips he had taken, without so much as a single nod to the National Book Award he received for *Buckdancer's Choice* in 1965, or that he'd been appointed Poetry Consultant at the Library

Of Congress in 1966. This was part of his ploy to give the public a surprise when it attended a poetry reading—those unfamiliar with him might arrive expecting the usual antiseptic evening, everyone formally dressed and nodding dutifully as the poet sowed his stuffy wisdom to the learned listeners. No, when Dickey entered a room for one of his readings, the intensity of his energy was so palpable that it was likely to arouse people to applause before he had even opened his mouth. Or, like my friend Chris, whistle loudly like he was at a football game or rock concert.

This was no run-of-the-mill poetry reading.

We sat on the second row, dead center, mere feet away from the man who then meant the whole world to us. Hard to believe it may be nowadays, but this poetry-loving audience numbered in the hundreds, the huge room packed, people clogging the aisles and standing along the walls. I could hardly keep my seat, such was the excitement I felt being so close to him. It was as if William Faulkner had walked into the room and stood right in front of me—it was that important. When Dickey began to read, his piercing concentrated enthusiasm put me on a virtual rollercoaster of emotional and intellectual sentiment. And, booming as his presentation could become at times, it also commanded the power to silence completely the people in attendance to the point of being able to hear yourself breathe or notice the beating of your own heart. This dichotomy was no better illustrated than during his recitation of the nostalgic poem, "Looking For The Buckhead Boys." It begins as a conventional quest for one's lost youth, as the now-middleaged narrator returns to the neighborhood of Buckhead where he was raised in search of the friends he once had there:

> *If I can find them, even one,*
> *I'm home. And if I can find him*
> *catch him in or around*
> *Buckhead, I'll never die: it's likely my youth will walk*
> *Inside me like a king.*

But beyond it's traditional introduction, Dickey allows the voices of the people to enter into the poem directly and, further, to speak boldly in their redneck vernacular, as when he recalls a favorite hangout the boys used to frequent, a filthy pool hall called Tyrees:

> *Charlie Gates used to say one of these days*
> *I'm gonna get myself the reputation of being*
> *The bravest man in Buckhead. I'm going in Tyree's toilet*
> *And pull down my pants and take a shit.*

This was *poetry*? Without a doubt. Perhaps of a different order than Wordsworth or Keats, but there was no mistaking the seriousness or the singular integrity of purpose behind Dickey's verse, even when it employed the crudities of down-home humor and left hundreds of people literally howling with laughter. The work I had read prior always impressed me with its courage, its willingness to push the parameters of what was "acceptable" in poetry, but seeing the work read by its creator caused this aspect to emerge in ways I never imagined. And when he finished this particular poem's final stanza, my friend and I fired one another a tacit glance I will never forget—in fact I cling to it, all these years later. For Chris' face was brightly splashed by a delicious astonishment I can hardly begin to describe the beauty of: the exhilarating, infectious life-awe some of us can't get enough of, the simple yet profound acknowledgment that, for those willing to put themselves out on one of the world's long limbs, *anything* was possible.

Can you believe it?

So out on the limb I went, easing myself just far enough to see what would happen, and the rest is history, my history. I began composing poems at what seemed to me an unheard-of rate, one a day typically but sometimes even two or three. Any spare second I had would go toward writing them: eating breakfast or riding the University transit bus to campus or sitting in a classroom awaiting the arrival of the professor. And once they began coming out it was all I could do to stop them: honestly, it was like they'd been in there the whole time, just waiting for me to pick up a pen and draw them out. Every afternoon I'd hurry home to my girlfriend Michelle and share with her the products of the day's efforts, and in no time at all started seeing signs of improvement—already the first batch of poems were beginning to show their age when compared with the work I was currently composing. But rather than being a source of discouragement, this actually fueled my determination, for it only served to illustrate how much better I could be if I continued to work at it. Forget mitosis, forget algorithms or political history—I'd finally found an *important* place for my energies.

That same year I signed up for an English course that advertised itself as a survey of 20th century American poetry: I needed to learn even more about who our great poets were and what it was they did, so I could see precisely where I might fit in once I joined their ranks. (Like many another college undergraduate, I didn't lack for ambition.) The instructor for that class was an unlikely professor named Coleman Barks, who looked to me like a wise old sage with a bushy black beard and a wild windy thicket of stormy dark hair. Not only did he assign poems by none other than James Dickey, he actually *knew* the man, was able to refer to him casually as a friend, Jim Dickey he'd say, and I'd shiver with envy from my seat in the second row. Arriving home that afternoon I hurriedly telephoned Chris in Connecticut to tell him the news, who responded to my gloating with appropriate proportions of irony and envy: he may have been attending one of the nation's top-ranked universities, but he couldn't begin to boast the unbelievable good fortune of having for a teacher a man who was actually friends with the living writer we then admired more than any other. 'You lucky bastard,' he said.

It need be noted here and now that meeting Coleman Barks has been as important as anything that has happened to me. Himself a poet of tremendous power, a badass by any standard, Coleman— nearly thirty years my senior—could not only match but actually surpass my youthful zest for poetry with his own, beyond which he also had one hell of a knack for making the ignoramus likes of an undergraduate feel as if he too could take part in the poetic process. Needless to say it took no time at all for me to burden the poor generous bard with my own fledgling efforts (horrified though I was when handing them to him), and some days later he gave me just the opportunity I needed to send me soaring: he enjoyed my poems, he said like a saint, and wondered if I might be interested in signing up for the Creative Writing course he'd be conducting the following quarter.

The class contained approximately fifteen students, and I'll confess that from the very start I saw all of them as competitors, not comrades. Fortunately, there were only a few among them who seemed to be half as serious about writing as I was, while the rest figured such a class would be an easy-enough alternative to writing term papers. On the first day, Coleman (as he insisted we call him, ditching a "Doctor's" formality) outlined his unorthodox grading method, admitting at the onset that he loathed the idea of "grading someone's creativity" but this was, after all, a college course, and University policy dictated that a student taking a class should be assigned a grade for the work he did there. The only way one could find himself with a final grade of F, Coleman said, was by refusing to write anything at all—a slim possibility. In all likelihood, he predicted with an assurance that scared me, A's were just as slim a possibility, as this grade was reserved for those who not only were prolific but also showed some special degree of talent and—most importantly—a dramatic improvement in their writing over the course of the quarter. The majority of the grades would therefore fall into the B and C range.

In his class, all of us sat around a big rectangular table, a first for me—classes typically were arranged like church, with the students as a lowly bunch of brainless nobodies sitting in rows before the priestly pedant up front, handing down the Great Knowledge like laws from on high. Although there were days during which we spent our time discussing the work of some already-established author, the majority were spent going over student efforts, with everyone offering opinions and suggestions while the poor writer minced around in his seat wondering why his piece wasn't perfect as written and waiting with bated breath to hear what Coleman would say. I took care to sift out who among my classmates were the ones offering sound, thoughtful advice, and in truth there were a few whose work was good enough to terrify me. But the sense of competitive goading became a challenge I relished: I worked on poems constantly, changing and reworking them and all the while learning without a hint of frustration that there were infinite ways to write a single thought or episode, the fun was finding the *best* way.

Approximately four weeks into the quarter I walked way out onto that long limb by asking Coleman if he might be willing to share with me James Dickey's mailing address so I could send him a letter—a fan letter, sure, but back then I never would have done myself the disservice of calling it that. Even though I was comfortable with Coleman in a way I had never before been with a teacher, I recall being a nervous wreck when I asked him for the favor, certain he would only scoff at my suggestion as the pipe-dream of a presumptuous student who was far more ambitious than he had any right to be. His response, however, was supportive and enthusiastic. Not only did he think it a good idea for me to send such a letter to "Jim," but why not send a sampling of my poems as well? And since he (Coleman) had been meaning to contact his old buddy, he thought he might go ahead and write a quick note to include in my package, which notion nearly caused me to collapse with gratitude right there in front of him. Not only did it assure me that he thought enough of my work to warrant the suggestion of sending it, but the fact that his letter would be part of the same package also assured me that Dickey would take the time to read mine, at least as a favor for a friend, not just drop it into a dusty pile of anonymous, unopened mail from his innumerable admirers.

I no longer have a copy of that first-ever fan letter, and feel confident I'd be disappointed and maybe even embarrassed by it were I able to have a look at what I wrote back then. Writing to one's hero is no small task—I'd wager it's the enormity of the endeavor that seems to discourage most of us from doing it more often. All I can say for certain regarding the contents of my letter is that it was an honest attempt to convey both my appreciation of Dickey's work and my damn-all determination to follow in his footsteps, neither of which was as simple to say as it should have been since one's passionate sincerity often threatens to sound like silly teenage fawning—not the way a "serious" writer wants to be seen. But I gave it my best, and carried it to Coleman along with the ten poems I'd selected to include so that, with luck, he'd stamp it all with his personal seal of approval. He did, and promised to have his letter completed and the entire package in the mail by week's end, subsequent to which I would endure for the very first time the element of sending away one's work for which there is no solace and no preparation: the agony of waiting.

Naturally an entire lifetime seemed to unfold in the weeks it took to receive a response. Every day I hurried home to the mailbox all excitedly hopeful, only to mope away despondent when nothing awaited me there. Seeing Coleman for class I made every effort to conceal from him the fact that I was being driven damn-near insane with anticipation, wondering how he could seem so calm and collected about the very thing that was making me a madman. All this, even though I didn't really expect much in the way of a response from what I'd sent—I only wanted to know that it was received, that he had read my letter and understood why I wrote it and would be grateful for my having actually taken the time to do so.

It was 1986, a Friday afternoon in February that was cold enough to warrant my wearing a heavy coat to class. Entering Park Hall, home of the English Department, I bumped into my friend Tucker, who wanted to know whether I might want to meet for a beer later that afternoon. I was on my way to Coleman's class and had one other still to attend subsequent to this one, but if he could hold out until around two-thirty he had himself a date. We picked a place downtown and said we'd see one another in a while, then I rushed on to class which was scheduled to have started five minutes prior. Just outside the door Coleman and I nearly ran into one another, he as tardy as I. 'Afternoon,' I said, and a big smile broke through his beard when he replied, 'I've got a good letter in here,' motioning to a notebook he was hugging to his chest. So I followed him into the classroom with a quick panic wreaking quiet havoc within me.

Once we were all situated around the table Coleman explained to everyone that he and I had 'sent some stuff to Jim Dickey,' and he had received a return letter that he thought he would share with the rest of us. I noted two empty seats . . . two slackards had skipped so would miss it. He began reading and I recall stealing one glance from Jody Cass, who looked at me as if to say *You sent something to James Dickey?* after which I froze my face in a downslant, scared shitless. The first half of his letter was directed strictly to Coleman and made no mention of me. I was listening, but also obsessing over what Coleman had said just before we walked into the classroom: 'I've got a good letter in here.' Innocent enough, not making me any promises. But then there was that smile . . . the smile was what I could not escape. It had set me up, said so much more than the sentence he'd uttered. Coleman said, 'I've got a good letter in here,' but the smile seemed to add, 'You're in for one-hell-of-a kick, my friend.' I was certain of it, had seen it with my own eyes. Hadn't I?

Which is when my name leapt out of the letter and grabbed me by the throat. I had a hard time swallowing, breathing. Coleman stopped for just a second and looked up at me . . . I suppose to make sure that I was paying attention. *You're in for one-hell-of-a kick, my friend.* Then he read on.

> *Tell him I will write him a separate letter when I get out from under a little of this necessary work; that I have not forgotten, nor will I pass him by. Tell him I think he is most extraordinarily gifted. If, as he says, I have had some effect on the way he writes, I have not spent my time for nothing: have not, in the language of telephonics and desperate mariners, been sending with a dead key. Ask Mr. Hanson if I may keep his poems, for living-with awhile. Tell him I think he is not far from a first book, and that when he is ready I have some suggestions.*

I swallowed, took a breath. Coleman read the last little bit but I hardly heard it, then it was quiet. Dead quiet. Who knows what the others were thinking, who knows what I was thinking? He handed the letter to me and said, 'Why don't you excuse yourself and go make a copy of this. In fact, why don't you make a *bunch* of copies.' He chuckled and smiled knowingly, and out the door I went.

Intuitively I focused on the task at hand—finding a photocopier—so as to stave the volcano building steam inside of me, threatening to blow and cause embarrassment. (In retrospect, I should have ripped off a rebel yell and run whooping through the church-quiet halls of the English Department—what good does it do to squelch one's excitement over something so significant as that letter was to me?) The secretary in the departmental office said I could use their machine to make a copy, but I cheated and made three: an extra for me, one for my mom, one for Chris. On the way back to class I reread three times the paragraph in which Dickey referred to me, a paragraph I would more or less memorize over the course of the next month, not from any concerted effort to do so but simply by virtue of having read it dozens of times.

Given what had gone down, it could've been tricky finding focus in class that day, but in fact Dickey's letter fired me up even more about what we were doing there. I remember we discussed poems by Melinda Hawley, whose work I believed to be of the highest order, and I felt badly for her, having to follow all of the letter excitement with those quiet, even-tempoed poems of hers. But read them she did, and accepted with no show of scorn the suggestions of classmates without a clue as to why her work was already alarmingly close to perfect. Which excited me even further, for suddenly I was starting to believe that we were *onto* something, that my classmates and I were on the cutting edge of literature's future. *Tell him I think he is not far from a first book*, the famous poet had written to me, so then surely the same could be said of those writers in the class toward whom I felt some kinship. It was as if we were given confirmation that the work we were doing *mattered* somehow, was leading us straight to a desired end that suddenly was in sight, and I wanted nothing more than to have company for the trek—perhaps with some prescience I perceived even then the lonely life that writing would demand of me, so wanted to share what of it I could while still able to do so. Melinda's poems managed to pry their way past all of my selfish excitement, and aroused my enthusiasm even more so that, by the time our class came to a close, I was damn-near explosive with ebullience, all the while quietly gathering my books as if it were just another day. Jody and Melinda and a couple of others approached to offer their kind congratulations, me basking in the first and only sense of fame I'd ever felt, but trying still for some silly reason to squelch it all and play it down as if it didn't make that much difference, was no big deal. Saying goodbye to Coleman my excitement must have leaked out a little around the edges because he said, 'It's fun, isn't it?'

Stepping outside the cold smacked me in the face and reminded me that I was awake and alive. It was 1986, a Friday afternoon in February on which I felt so immeasurably magnificent that I actually was able to forget it was all ephemeral, was even then escaping from me like Time. I decided without a second thought to skip my next class . . . wander around downtown a bit before meeting Tucker for what by now had become a celebratory beer. Across from Wuxtry, the record shop where I spent most of the money I didn't have in those days, was a pay telephone, so that's where I headed, hoping first to catch my mom, then Chris. I moved at a pace nearer a jog than a walk, with the photocopied letter—which I'd read twice more since leaving Park Hall, admiring the personalized letterhead, my hero's name and address emblazoned at the top—burning a hole in my hand. It was happening . . . *all* of it . . . everything was happening. The world was opening itself up before me, *me*, the little red-headed runt of a so-called writer who never excelled in anything was *not far from a first book*! And, as if there were no limit to what the day could provide, I actually succeeded in reaching both of the people with whom I so desperately wanted to share the fun.

Which is the one aspect of the memory that causes me regret, now that it's reduced to retrospection. Though the particulars of what was said during my conversation with Chris have long escaped me, I can vividly recall the one thing that was not said, even when it should have been the first thought to leave my lips: Thank you. Thank you for showing me, opening my eyes. Thank you for coaxing me to the Colony Book Shop where I grudgingly paid seven dollars for a collection of poems by some guy named Dickey I'd never even heard of; for contriving a snake-hunting excursion with something so antiquated as a blowgun and making me believe it was important we were doing it; for making the trek to Athens, where we'd lay eyes on our hero for the first time; and finally for convincing me, with all the false conviction you could summon, that it could happen to *us*, that *we* could be the admired ones to alight hope in the heart of some shrimp of a kid who may never make six feet in height but might one day write a great book in spite of the fact. *The letter I hold in my hand would not be here were it not for you, my friend, and for that I thank you.*

No, this was not the tone our conversation would take. I was too busy reeling from success, a first-ever sense of myself as someone to whom things could happen, someone who could accomplish something, something huge and impressive—thus would have to live with the sad fact of that neglect forever after. I was just so *excited*, you see. How could I know I would lose that chance? We were *kids*, for Christ's sake, with nothing but Time stretching out forever in front of us like a future whose script we could write for ourselves. I had it all figured out, and how could I have imagined how different the world would be within five short years—that, among other things ever more tragic, I'd be no closer to publishing that promised first book and still searching in vain for the enormous elusive Something that would make me feel good about myself?

Though I wasn't cognizant of it at the time, hindsight has since convinced me that our camping/canoe trip was a kind of test of my initiative, one of those all-too-rare occasions on which I actually concocted a crazy scheme myself rather than waiting on someone more capable—like Chris—to take the lead and do it for me, for all of us.

I was newly graduated from college and living in Chapel Hill, North Carolina, sharing an apartment with my long-time friend Lamar, part of the Savannah gang that got drunk, argued the merits of movies, laughed, performed in plays, and made our own 8-millimeter "masterpieces"—the gang that included Chris and our other favored friend Mark, who by then had fathered a son and was settling quietly into family life . . . against our wishes. Chris was still a student, now in the Creative Writing program at Columbia University in New York. Three days subsequent to my receiving final grades, Lamar drove down to Athens to move me up to his place in Chapel Hill, where we hoped like hell we could hammer-out film screenplays together as a team. This is what I had announced to my parents on a trip home just months prior, sitting in the sunroom of our house with my voice shaking: I was fully prepared for them to crucify my plan with pragmatics, shoot down the dream by endeavoring to convince me that writing wasn't the kind of thing most people would call a "career", and wouldn't I consider something a bit more financially reliable for my future. But I was way off: my mother and stepfather offered nothing but support for that pipe-dreaming son of theirs, saying I'd be sorry if I didn't "give it a try" and would henceforth live out my life mired in regret and wondering *What if . . . ?* Lamar still had one more semester of classes to complete for graduation, but I went ahead and moved to his neck of the woods and got busy working by myself, shifting my focus from poems to short stories, fiction. And never stopped.

Lamar and I shared a gig as managers/projectionists at a local movie-house (a real one, before it was necessary to add *retro* to the title), but this excluded Lamar from our canoe trip because we couldn't both go and leave the theatre in the lurch. Chris wanted to go, too, but now that he was all the way up the coast in New York it simply wasn't feasible for him to come down. So the group that ended up going included Mark, Chris's younger brother Paddy, and Craig, a more recent addition to our antics who was older than the rest of us by roughly a decade, all three of whom drove up together from Savannah on a Thursday night so we could begin our adventure first thing Friday morning. I signified the start by popping in a videocassette of the movie *Deliverance* at four-thirty a.m., so it'd be the backdrop while we packed our supplies: the video's colors had become muted and its picture had gone grainy from a relentless repetition of viewings. Mark and I both knew the movie by heart (for an entire summer he and Chris joked about figuring a way to splice the film so it would run continuously on a loop, such was the seriousness of our obsession— whenever we all got together that summer we eventually ended up watching it, typically at two or three in the morning with eyes blurried from booze), so could successfully quote all of the dialogue along with the characters. Mark's mimicry of the accents was hilariously uncanny, and the last line he uttered before we switched off the set to start our journey was, 'Sometimes you have to lose yourself, before you can find *anything*.'

The drive home after our trip was more of the same, fun and good talk. But, for me at least, there was a lot of sadness just beneath the surface. We had finally done it, that which had been secretly inscribed on my private agenda for the past two years, the groped-after experience that I thought would never happen simply because I wanted it to so badly. We did it and now it was over and done with, a thing of the past.

"But the river underlies, in one way or another, everything I do." *I suppose that the only way to cope with one's memories, and the sad nostalgic longing that always accompanies them, is to make new ones—spend one's entire life in a determined ceaseless search for that Something New under the sun rather than relying on the same old tried and true ones to make you happy. If I cast our weekend in metaphoric terms, wrenched it for the ramifications that make me sad, I would say that our violent spill on the first set of rapids we faced—me in a tumbling fit being banged-up by big murderous rocks—held my mortality in front of me as if on a movie screen, and that this realization has caused me to see my life like a long rollercoaster river cluttered with stones threatening to impede safe passage. And that, ultimately, I'll be broken apart by one of those stones, and sink out of sight.*

But if I allow the trip to stay in my first mind, where it originated and took place, I would say simply that it was a wonderful, adventure-blessed weekend that—try though I may—will never be duplicated.

This, from an account I wrote and titled, aptly but derivatively, *Desperately Seeking Deliverance*: on the title page I penned a dedication to James Dickey, almost as if I believed someone would publish the piece. It was composed in one thrilling six-week concentration of effort just subsequent to our going: a trip that transpired exactly as I had wanted it to, with the notable exception of our awful accident on the very first set of rapids, Patton's Run, a frothy, rough-riding stretch that's like descending a bumpy set of stone steps in a boat. It was a weekend that would not have happened were it not for me—I *created* it, made virtually all of the arrangements myself so the guys need only agree to go and it would be there waiting when they showed up. And in truth the bad accident helps make the whole weekend that much more memorable, for we were in the spray-filled center of a violent drama that threatened our safety and even garnered us a great deal of attention from other people paddling the river that day. Granted, I would have rather ridden right through those rapids unscathed and without a hitch, for it was frightening and physically painful as well (at the time I believed I had broken my leg but it was only badly bruised). Still, all these years after the fact, the terrifying excitement of that accident is the first thing that comes to mind whenever one of us mentions the trip to the others—it really stays with me, whereas I can't even recall which leg was all beat-up because of it.

Michelle and I moved to Atlanta the following year. Having just finished my first novel and started work on a second, now I was residing in the very same city in which my favorite living writer was raised. Though Lamar would later relocate there as well, it was no longer with any notion of writing screenplays with me: by then we were both resigned to doing our own work, which didn't include for either of us the shrinking of literary aspirations to fit what I now considered the meretricious demands of movie-making. Michelle was looking to get into Social Work, I was looking to get whatever job I could just so long as it allowed me to write. And write I did. Write and write and write. Not forsaking the ascetic regimen I had imposed on myself the minute I moved to Chapel Hill, I continued to rise at five every morning without fail to pursue the vague pleasures of being a novelist before the sun rose up and the phone started to ring. I'd finish up around eight, grudgingly descend to the dreaded real-world requirements we're all condemned to endure, working for a while at a catering company and then later securing something a bit more stable by accepting an office job on the campus of Georgia State University. At five in the afternoon I would herd myself onto the subway same as everyone else, and, arriving home by five-thirty, fix a pot of coffee to stir the waning after-work spirits so for the second time that day I could sit myself down behind the cardtable I called my desk and—conjuring my life in terms Dickey made famous—try to buy back a bit of my soul by doing the work that mattered most to me. These were the days, I am now well aware, when I concretized the course my life was to take forever after . . . when certain habits became set in the very marrow, so I could no longer imagine my life without them. Between the full-time job and the manuscripts that monopolized my attention, I was working very long hours, sometimes sixteen and seventeen per, ablaze with ambition and the seemingly endless juice of the 23-year-old. And although the professional aspects of writing (namely publishing) left me more than a little malnourished, my soul was anything but—I was in hot pursuit of that silent but immense satisfaction, one that left me feeling like nothing less than the luckiest guy in the whole wide world, a man after God's own heart. It was quite a place to come to, where I felt a sense of hope and purpose that left me almost giddy, created a sense of confidence I never knew possible prior to arriving there.

Let's call it Dickeyland.

I had not heard from the famous author since the reading I'd attended—*sans* Chris—only a few months following the receipt of his letter: it was conducted at a small college outside of Atlanta, conveniently occurring during our spring break. So I made the trek with a friend, who spent most of the time trying to tap my courage so I'd approach the man, remind him who I was. Which I did, shaking his hand after the reading and reminding him that I'd written to him through Coleman Barks some years back, and he stared me straight in the eye with a scary look of seriousness and said, 'You're a good writer, Mr. Hanson, and that's no bullshit. I'm not here to bullshit you.' These were the first words out of his mouth, the first words he ever said to my face, and they left me limp-kneed, thinking I'd drop dead of happiness on the spot.

At a mid-afternoon panel discussion with three other poets, he graciously inflated my ego even further by addressing issues or questions raised by the audience before turning to me—wide-eyed in the front row—to say, 'Wouldn't you agree, Mr. Hanson? Don't you find that to be true of your work?' to which I would casually nod in quiet confirmation, as if the circumstance of this famous writer including me in his conversation was something that happened all the time, wasn't causing such a commotion within me that I thought I might be sick to my stomach. And this wasn't the last of the day's beneficent surprises. When the discussion ended, Dickey asked me if we'd like to join him for the "closed" luncheon immediately to follow, which my friend and I did, me drifting through the whole affair as if in a dream, waiting on someone to shake me and say it was time to wake up. I sat right beside Dickey but said next to nothing, too nervous to contribute to the conversation and awed by being so close to him, and an hour later we said our goodbyes so as to make the drive back before nightfall. He told me to stay in touch and let him know how my work was progressing, then shook my hand and walked away. My cup runneth over. It never even occurred to me that I'd been the shortest guy in the room.

Two years later, relocated to Atlanta, the opportunity to see him again would present itself on a couple of occasions, wherein I could—were I again able to summon courage from its safe slumber—avail myself for some of his time now that he knew not only my name but also my face, not to mention had some small fondness for the work I was doing . . . or so he had said. Of course, these opportunities had always been available, but living in North Carolina I never heard about them: no one I met there seemed much interested in James Dickey, who most people knew only as "the guy who wrote *Deliverance*." All of the local writers were revered and talked-about, but beyond the boundaries of the state no other writers seemed to exist. Even though South Carolina was the state in which Dickey had made his home since the late sixties, Atlanta still claimed him as one of its favorite sons, consequently any time the man made an appearance anywhere near the city, or within the state, for that matter, newspapers and magazines made a fuss about it like it like seeing him was the chance of a lifetime.

No denying it was, and I was no less aware of the fact for having already faced it: what little of Dickey's time I was fortunate to have had was just enough to make me yearn for more of it, especially now that I was starting to accept the notion of myself as a writer, a *real* writer—not necessarily an equal to someone of Dickey's stature, but at least someone who was mirroring his example with a certain seriousness, one I was starting to see as exceptional since more than a few people I'd known to be aspiring writers had long ago given up on the notion and were going back to school in droves to obtain a teaching degree. Although I'd been given a vote of confidence from the man and writer I admired most; completed two of Coleman's creative writing courses (the second a graduate-level course—I was the only undergrad) with lots of compliments and A's in both of them; even published a few of my poems in little-known college quarterlies that not only accepted my work but actually *paid* me for it ($50.00 apiece for two of my poems . . . the first and last money I have made from writing), all in advance of my twenty-third birthday, *still* I had difficulty calling myself as a writer. And naturally this is what I desired more than anything else at the time—I *needed* it, so set out to satisfy this one simple goal that can prove to be so slippery, especially starting out.

My formula for cauterizing this damnable insecurity was to ratchet-up my commitment with a die-hard discipline I'd never devoted to anything, certainly not school. I set the alarm for five every morning and dragged myself out of bed as if there were something tangibly valuable to gain from having done so, and less than a year later I had completed—and collected rejections for— over a dozen short stories, also finished my first novel, a task of which I never imagined myself capable. I had just turned twenty-four when I started a second book, still wondering if I *really* was a writer. Believe me when I say that I recognize the pointlessness of this particular anxiety, but the so-called validity some sort of professional success can bestow upon a career is difficult to deny, and carrying on without such a thing requires a stamina of faith that's far from simple to sustain. But I was working my ass off in spite of this concern, or perhaps *because* of it, and the sixteen-hour days did nothing to drain the abundance of creative energy my ambition lent me. I hated having to *sleep*, resented giving up my conscious hours when I could be riding that rush, and even the rejections I regularly received for my fiction served only to fan the determined flames I felt burning within me. *Let's be the new gods*, Chris used to write at the close of his letters—my feeling then was that we were well on our way to becoming just that.

When I learned there was going to be a writer's conference in Charleston, South Carolina, and that Dickey was one of the artists the conference was proudly boasting as a participant, I actually considered shunning the opportunity for the fear that being around "real" writers might deflate the illusion of myself as one of them. At this point I was approximately three-quarters of the way through my second novel (or such was my estimation, based more on instinct than some sort of actual outline), and had hit a hard stretch where I wasn't exactly certain how to enact what I'd decided I wanted for the book's ending. My pre-dawn work began to stall, became an agony: I'd sit for two-and-a-half hours with less than a paragraph to show for my efforts, and for the rest of the day would deprecate myself over the lack of progress that morning. In the evenings I was dictating my hand-written pages to an angelic soul named Hillary, a friend from college who also was living in Atlanta and had agreed to type the book for me since she had access to a word processor (the cutting-edge technology in those days), and she was the one who pushed me to take a week off to attend the conference. What harm could it do, she wanted to know, when the work wasn't going so well anyway?

What I decided to do was compromise: I wouldn't register for any of the conference classes (all of which required payment of some kind), but would drive down just for the weekend so as to attend the readings that were offered openly to the general public. Michelle said she'd take the weekend off to accompany me, so on a sunny Friday morning we set out on our way, me still fending more than a fair share of guilt for going to see other writers when I should be staying home to work, staying home to *be* a writer.

Rumor had it that most of the "major" writers were staying in a big hotel called The Mills House, but by the time we arrived the place was already booked to capacity so we were forced to go find less ambitious lodgings. It wasn't as easy as I'd hoped, the conference drawing a much larger crowd than I had anticipated, consequently most of the inns and hotels in the downtown area were without vacancies. But on our fourth stop we managed to wrangle a room, only, according to the woman at the front desk, because they'd just had a cancellation, so our timing turned out to be fortuitous.

Once we'd checked-in and dumped our stuff upstairs, we headed to where the action was, at least that's how I saw it: if all of the writers were staying at the Mills House, then by god that's where we needed to be. I may have claimed our reason for coming was only to attend the readings, but in reality I still had my hopeful heart set on another meeting with Dickey, and—who knows?— maybe even one or two other writers I admired on the conference roster (meaning my agenda was pretty much the same as every other young writer attending). Which isn't to say I was there just to "network" (a repugnant verb in any vocabulary), strategically making connections with successful people so as to give myself a career-boost—I was far too naïve to buy into the belief that such a thing mattered. For better or worse, thus began a pattern I would later find myself unable to break, meeting writer after writer who perhaps could have helped me in some professional way were I to put myself out and ask. Instead, I refused to compromise what I saw as infinitely more valuable, not to mention enjoyable: namely the potential soul-connection I might be able to strike, the companionship of someone who already had been where I was, so might recognize exactly what I was going through to write those books of mine, all the joy and fear and conflict moving within me, and how writing had become a means to reaching out, reminding others they weren't alone—lots of us are living with a buried reality. I hadn't learned yet that if these writers wanted to meet people, find new friendships for themselves, it probably wasn't with young nobodies who had nothing beyond friendship to offer—those people who, were they given the opportunity, might just have the talent to steal away whatever spotlight these supposed superiors had managed to secure over the years.

When we arrived at the Mills House, I went first to check the bar— where else would my heroes be?—but struck out. So we decided just to wander a bit, see who we might happen upon. I was a nervous wreck, but Michelle god love her kept reminding me that, at least with regard to Dickey, I had already broken the ice and should have no qualms about approaching him. She was right, of course, but that made it no easier. My first meeting with him had been nearly a year prior, hence my concern for the moment was that he would have absolutely no memory of me whatsoever, regardless of the letter I'd written him in the interim. This was a man who met more people in a day than I did in months, and as far as letters go I could hardly conceive of the countless numbers of strangers who might pen fan-letters to him. Why would he bother to remember me, of all those?

Across the lobby from the front desk was a bookstore, so I left Michelle looking at a painting and beelined to it, seeking the safe refuge of a place where I could appear to be searching for writers, when in fact I was burying myself in books so I wouldn't have to bother. The first thing I confronted was one of those tall rotating racks on which popular paperbacks are displayed, and that is why I did not spot Dickey standing behind it until I'd nearly bumped into him. I was speechless, but like a hero he bailed me out.

'I owe you a letter,' he said, extending his hand.

I had just exhausted my stock of innocuous chit-chat regarding the drive when he suggested we get a drink in the bar since he had some time to kill. 'I was just looking for something junky to read,' he said. With trepidation I confessed that I was accompanied by my girlfriend, figuring that'd be it, he'd brush me off and mosey on to some more-available admirer. Instead he said, 'I'll meet you two in the bar,' and off I went.

Michelle might be better qualified than I am to write the rest of what transpired that afternoon. For me, Time seemed first to freeze, then leap, and what I was left with was three-and-a-half hours of terrified bliss and a hangover. Contrary to all the media talk about Dickey slowing down and sobering up, talk for which he himself was responsible, I watched in confused amazement while that man pounded double martinis for three solid hours, me playing it somewhat safer by drinking mugs of dark beer. I say "somewhat" because in truth I did everything in my power to match his drinking, keep up with him, suckered into the textbook fallacy that my seriousness as an artist could be conveyed by my capacity for alcohol—by the end of our visit I had gone well beyond my limit and would end up crashing before eight o'clock that evening. But such was no matter, as I saw it: I had an opportunity to get gloriously drunk with a hero, and I was not about to let it go. There even were moments during the course of our conversation when I was allowed the luxury of a wonderful self-awareness: some stranger would stop to shake the celebrity's hand, say how much he admired his work, and the reality of my situation would strike me suddenly and I would just reel from it, stealing glances at Michelle that said, *Can you believe this is happening?* to which she would slyly smile back with eyes shining, *Of course I can!* I would watch Dickey deal cordially with the people who were interrupting us to introduce themselves, and relish the fact I was there sitting with him, *right there*, not interrupting his conversation with some other lucky bastard who'd look at me with a mixture of pity and self-satisfaction. It was, quite literally, as crazy a circumstance as I could have conjured.

You would think there might have been awkward lulls in our talking, since over thirty years of experience separated us, but such wasn't the case at all—there was so much I wanted to ask him about that I could hardly get my thoughts out quickly enough, afraid I would forget something. And what was most surprising is that this fantasy didn't play itself out like an interview, with the young Hopeful firing-off one question after another to the wise old superior. On the contrary, Dickey did nothing if not make every effort to treat me as an equal, and the only time it became blatantly obvious that our private intellects were light-years apart was when he'd launch into a recitation of some obscure Latin passage to illustrate a point he meant to make, or likewise recite entire stanzas in French from a favorite poet, Paul Valéry. Otherwise we conversed as if we were comrades, Dickey often responding to my queries by shooting them right back at me— wanting to know *my* work habits or asking me to elucidate for him *my* preference for a particular writer.

When I confessed the frustration I was then facing for the first time regarding the writer's inability to work something to a state of perfection, he gave some simple advice that I'd spend the rest of my writing life reminding myself: 'You may not be able to get it perfect,' he said, staring me straight in the eye and becoming deadly serious, 'but you can get it *close*.' When he asked what were the titles of the two books I was then working on, I actually hesitated: I'd never told anyone my titles before . . . it seemed such a huge step to take since they weren't yet set in stone. But this was a day for such steps so tell him I did, and awaited his condemnation with a quivering ego. Meaning my paranoia was alive and well. *Among Trees*, the title of my first novel, he honestly appeared to be taken with, so much so that he brought it up again later, confirming his approval by saying, 'That's *good*.'

We spent time talking about the projects he was currently involved with, particularly his latest novel, *Alnilam*, about which he was still very excited. By this date, Dickey had more or less dismantled most of the hype he'd built-up around his book-poem *The Zodiac*, a work whose moments of genuine insight powerfully rendered were undermined and eventually overshadowed completely by disastrously drunken descents into self-aggrandizement. But *Alnilam*, a big sprawling book some thirty years in the making, was another matter. I told him how much I admired the book, one that—for all its faults—proved once again that Dickey was not at all interested in repeating himself, and was a true heir to Faulkner's notion that a novelist's supreme aim was to write a noble failure. This is perhaps the greatest lesson I learned from Dickey's example, or at least it made him as distinct from other writers as did his written voice: that one should constantly challenge himself by doing something completely different with each book he sought to write, and this could be accomplished by way of changing voices, experiments in structure, literary gymnastics. This was the writer's only means to growth, the best way in which to reinvent not only a reader's interest in the work but also his own. Dickey's poetry had proven this personal proclivity for change time and time again, sometimes to his readers' chagrin— one typically prefers a certain "type" of poetry over another, hence wishes the poet would stick with that particular style rather than spiraling off into experimentation. And like it or not

Alnilam confirmed that his approach to fiction was no different. Unlike the protagonist of the bestselling *Deliverance*, this novel's narrator was a far cry from the smart, affable, sensitive sort of fellow we followed through the first book—he was inarticulate and unemotional, more visceral than intellectual, and he was blind, to boot. To make matters even worse (for readers wanting a repeat performance), rather than employing what the author himself referred to as the straightforward, stripped-down style of *Deliverance*, *Alnilam* was wordy and voluminous in its stylistic scope, sometimes splitting its perspective straight down the page to reflect simultaneously the world through sighted eyes and also that experienced by his blind protagonist. The book was—to say the least—an ambitious follow-up to Dickey's previous fictional effort, and he dearly paid the price for his daring, publicly via poor sales, and critically via mixed, lukewarm reviews.

But the man was *excited* . . . you would have thought he'd written another *Moby Dick*.

It honestly hadn't occurred to me there might be some amount of pressure exerted on him, from within and without, to deliver a *Deliverance* sequel, but Dickey made it clear to me that day not only how simple such a thing would be from a writing standpoint, but also how much money could be made from a professional one. *This is a man with a family to support*, I found myself thinking, remembering him as human all of a sudden, one of us.

'I guess it's hard to avoid,' I mused aloud, 'writing *Deliverance II* just for the money,' half joking as though he'd probably never considered any such nonsense. But his smile vanished in an instant and a look of sad resignation stole over him when he said, 'You have no *idea* how hard.'

Three-and-a-half of the finest hours of my life raced by in this manner, and when we stood to say goodbye, shaking hands and saying our *Thank you*s, I felt truly connected to that man in some way, might even be thought of as a friend. Tipping the generous scale, he said to please let him know if there was anything he could do for me as far as my work went, and pressed me to stay in touch, keep him posted on my progress. After which that towering figure turned and walked away, the huge hulk of him seemingly unshaken by the enormous intake of gin—a physical memory firmly implanted, but one that would later become cruelly juxtaposed with the painful one I was to acquire on our final visit together, when Dickey's phthisis left little doubt that any day could be his last.

The Atlanta apartment Michelle and I were sharing at this time was called a one-and-a-half bedroom, the half being a small room that Michelle generously sacrificed so I could call it my office. The room offered just enough space for the cardtable-desk I use to this day, a stack of four filing drawers, and room on the floor for me to lay myself flat in order to stretch my back when I'd been working for a while and had begun stiffening rigidly to the h-contours of my chair. On the walls I tacked pictures of my heroes at the time—Dickey, filmmaker Bob Fosse, my mom— and, just to the right of the doorway as you entered, a large piece of white posterboard on which I had created a calendar: twelve months reduced to six-inch rectangles, 365 days squeezed to one-inch squares within each month. Every day when I finished working I would count the number of words I had written and pen the number on the corresponding square of the calendar, above which a quotation was inscribed in all-caps on an index card: SO AS NOT TO KID MYSELF. The line was uttered by Hemingway, from whom I'd copped this method of keeping track of my writing habits, a strategy I'd started using immediately subsequent to college graduation and one I continue to employ all these years later (though I no longer use the oversized posterboard). Under my bed at this very moment, however, three pieces of this dusty posterboard are pressed between paintings I have not enough wall-space to hang, and if I extract those cardboard calendars I can see exactly how much I accomplished in my first three years as a committed novelist. I like looking at them every now and then, for the fact is I accomplished quite a lot in those fiery young years when the world was so full of possibilities I couldn't keep count of them all. The squares are drawn with black magic-marker and the word-counts written in red, the inks of each fading just as fast now as my memory of that time. I was hard on myself, and kept those calendars "publicly" displayed on my wall so that anyone who came to our apartment would see them, therefore motivating me to fill-up those little squares with something other than embarrassing red zeros. There are zeros present, of course, because I refused with a die-hard honesty I still feel good about to lie when I was lazy, so whenever forced to put a zero on a particular day I would work that much harder on all the days subsequent so as to overshadow my shameful failure and the awful red-inked proof of it. (There is even a month in which I apparently wrote not one single word, and the sententious young side of me wrote in big bold letters that take up the entire six-inch rectangle, WASTED DUE TO LAZINESS. God only knows where my mind was that month—the grace is that I've forgotten.) There is something else, too: below the word-count for each day, a square may also contain an asterisk, depending on whether I took the time to do my daily exercises and go for a four-mile run, so that in effect every single facet of my life was thus reduced to a discipline, and every discipline had its roots in my writing. If I skimped on any one of them I was not a "real writer," thus could give up the notion of my name being added to the canon of literary history alongside those I revered.

The strategy succeeded, at least work-wise. The sight of those zeros successfully shamed me into shutting that door and getting down to work, though anyone with eyes could see that I was beginning to become more obsessed with history-making than could be considered healthy, alienating most of my friends and living with a woman I loved dearly but rarely took the time to talk to. How Michelle lived with it remains a mystery.

'If you want me to be honest with you,' a close friend confessed years later, referring to this period of my writing life, 'you had become *inaccessible*.'

It's simple math: those sixteen-hour days left little time for any sort of social life, and the wear-and-tear on my relationships began to take a serious toll, though at the time I devoutly refused to recognize it. All that I could see was what my ambition held as hope before me, and since I saw myself more or less as a loser, a runt whose intellectual prowess was sadly commensurate to that of his inferior physical stature, I believed that the only chance I had of rising from the dubious ranks of the lemmings to the glorious heights of my heroes was determination and discipline . . . WILL. Back when he'd quoted the heights of his heroes in that letter, Chris had planted within my heart the notion that would eventually become the driving force in my life—namely, the desire to distinguish myself in spite of obvious shortcomings, an idea I'm certain was subtly adopted during my late teens, and to which I became *fiercely* committed after college graduation. Among other things, the drunken afternoon with Dickey served only to inflame these obsessions even further.

Using those old posterboard calendars, it's easy to calculate the intoxicating effects of that visit. The triumphant days of the trip are marked on the weekend of September 9-12 with the initials CWC—Charleston Writer's Conference—and the numbers immediately subsequent reflect the surge of energy and enthusiasm I felt after spending some time with the writer I so revered: there are many days during this stretch when my word-count exceeded a thousand—a rarity really, as my average typically hovered around the 200-300 mark. It was this big push that finished for me my second novel, and, still reeling from all the excitement over the visit and the adrenaline that accompanied it, I plunged headlong into a third book without so much as a second thought regarding what I should be doing in order to see the previous two published. These were the days when I had to make hardly any effort whatsoever to rise above the agonizing insecurities provoked by publishing: I believed with all my heart that I was building a body of the most passionate fiction on the planet, only the world wasn't aware of it yet. Once I was ready, however, I would hand those books over to the publisher, who would have been waiting with bated breath all along to help me make history, and that would be that . . . next thing I'd know some young wannabe, crippled by doubt because of height or red hair, would be writing letters to *me*, telling me how my work had changed their life, motivated them to move beyond the borders they imagined imprisoned them and pour all of their pain and joyful passion into something so magnificent as a novel.

This was the way the world worked—you slaved over something until you succeeded, reached that vague goal you'd always known was out there waiting for you, then sat back to reap the beneficent rewards of your efforts. I had it all figured out, everything, and I was only twenty-five.

I was roughly fifty pages into the third novel when I went to visit Coleman Barks for a weekend, excitedly making the one-hour drive from Atlanta to the college town in which I'd endured over four years of student life, and on that Saturday night the two of us took turns reading aloud from the projects on which we were then working. I read first, stumbling along somewhat sloppily due to the hasty slanted script of my cursive which was more than a little difficult to decipher but satisfied my Dickey-induced desire to keep the task of writing as primitive as I could—'Writing should involve as little machinery as possible,' he'd said. Also I was extremely nervous: I'd not shared my work in this manner since college, now three years prior, and in that time had worked without any sort of guidance or influence whatsoever, a method that by then had become recondite, as the majority of published writers were the product of some high-powered writing program churning out poets and novelists like other programs produced doctors and lawyers. But read I did, my terrified tongue loosening-up a little once I'd gotten past the first couple of pages and began to become captured by what I had written, rolling right along as if the text was emerging spontaneously at that very moment, and even wondering myself where the story was going to go.

It was before I'd finished ten pages that Coleman stopped me in mid-sentence and said, 'This is a first draft?' his tone incredulous enough to confuse me. I went on to read another three or four pages before he stopped me again, saying, 'You're not my student anymore,' to which I wasn't sure how to respond until he added, 'You've left me and Dickey behind. The voice I'm hearing belongs to somebody else . . . somebody brand new,' and I felt something break open inside of me and blossom as a big stupid smile stretching the full width of my face. I'll never forget the feeling I had that night, for Coleman was convincing me that I was not just some crazy naive pipe-dreamer, that it actually was within my capacity to *do* the things I wanted to do with my life. And I was beginning to believe him, was able to open arms outward and accept myself, to embrace who I was as someone with something to offer rather than the self-loathing little twerp who had nothing within him worthy of giving. *I can do it, I really can*, I seemed to be thinking. After all, could someone as qualified as Coleman really be wrong about me?

The letter wasn't my idea, so when I wrote to Dickey with the request I said as much right at the onset: *Coleman suggested I write to you . . .*

By this time I had hit what I estimated to be the half-way point of the new novel, on which I worked every morning while in the evenings busied myself making revisions on the first two. What I wrote to request was whether he might be willing to write for me a letter of recommendation, something I could submit to publishers along with my manuscripts in the hopes that they might then be more inclined to *read* the stuff rather than just attach the standard rejection slip and return the material unconsidered. I was completely ignorant of the ways in which one should approach publishers, and this sounded like sort of a longshot, one Dickey might even resent me for making. But Coleman seemed to think it was just what I needed, so I trusted him as a superior, screwed my courage to the sticking place and sent the letter as suggested. Then I got back to the business at hand: my third novel, whose convoluted narrative was taking me farther out onto that long limb than I'd ever gone before.

What struck me as strange when I pulled it from the mailbox was that the response arrived in a big manila envelope, not just folded three-ways into the standard letter sort, so for the first time since sending the request I actually felt hopeful. Opening the package I found two letters, the first addressed to me, the other *To whom it may concern.* I read the personal one first, in which he suggested I use the enclosed letter with my submissions, also that I have Coleman write a similar one as well: *For Coleman is a fine writer himself, and his name would be very meaningful in this connection, I'm certain.* Then he made some other thoughtful comments, one concerning something I'd discussed with him before because it was an issue to which I was giving serious consideration, and I wanted every opinion on the subject I could get—marriage. Michelle and I had been together for over six years, half of which were spent sharing the same livingspace, and since marriage was something she felt strongly about I was thinking I should do it for her, regardless of the fact that I was perfectly content with our arrangement the way it was. Dickey, not surprisingly (since he was by then deep into his second marriage), was all gung-ho about my going through with it: *It's the only true state, I'm convinced,* he wrote. *That way you have something to build, and someone to build it with.*

But the closing comments were what sent me into orbit, for they seemed to hint at a future that would always involve him in some way, one in which he would be there for me through the worst: *My best to you, Red-head. Let me know how all this comes out, and regardless of anything and everything, I will back your play.* This was what I had to look forward to . . . a hero for a cheerleader . . . and what could possibly be better than that? Again, it was incredible how utterly *simple* life seemed, how gracious and giving it could be for those willing to make some sacrifices and put in some hard work. Here it was, all of it happening, all of those extraordinary things I didn't even realize I wanted until they were right there in front of me and—my god!—I hadn't even read his recommendation yet.

It hangs in an old black metal frame that I found collecting dust in my mother's laundry room back home, and right beside it is tacked a dirty yellow hospital band with my name on it, a remnant from an accident that could have killed me, but didn't— from the seat at which I have spent all the years of my writing life, they hang to my immediate left and I see them both for roughly three hours every single morning. What a life we have. I could not have imagined back then that receiving this gorgeous letter—in which the writer I most admire speaks of my work as if it is special, significant—would mark the beginning of a slow downward spiral that would send me not only to near-death in a hospital, but also through a divorce followed by the death and funeral for perhaps the most remarkable friend I'd ever have. So much happens within me whenever I look at that framed letter—it releases so much joy and hope and anguish, so much painful memory, so much astonishing awe at the unfathomable mystery of our miraculous lives, that you'd never know it was only ink stamped into shapes on an aging piece of paper, yellowed a little more each day on its way to disintegration despite all of my glass-framed efforts to preserve it forever.

Excited beyond my capacity to keep it, I immediately mailed Chris a copy of the letter, and though some part of him was obviously happy for me another side was sadly envious, figuring that such should have been *his* due, since he was the one initially responsible for our hero-worship, and even had written to Dickey just as I had done but without the benefit of going through a personal acquaintance in the way that I'd gone through Coleman. Welcome to the way of the world—Lesson 1.

And even though it had always seemed completely clear to me how personally responsible Chris was for turning my misguided life around and getting me involved with the world in a positive way, I'd never really *said* as much, actually told him how grateful I felt. So I suppose he might have remained uncertain, felt unappreciated, hence there was no avoiding the serrated jealous streak that eventually surfaced between us—especially since we were both writers and wanted to make our unique marks, naturally one of us was bound to have some luck before the other one. While I knew all along that *he* was the one with the greatness to get anything he wanted, perhaps even the *genius* to do so, some insecure side of him I never saw must have wondered whether the world was going to play an awful joke on him by dropping success into *my* lap, even though I'd still be wandering around without a clue had he not been there to give me some guidance. Friends may sincerely want for one another, but they want for themselves first—Lesson 2.

Privately, the complications were not so profound for me; they were, however, no less difficult to deal with. Fact is, once I'd received that letter I became *obsessed* with getting my work published. Here I had written two novels and half of a third without really sweating (too much) the rejections I'd received, more concerned with just getting the work done, then all of a sudden I imagine I've got a guarantee. So when I submit my manuscripts with Dickey's recommendation enclosed and *still* get shot-down? What the hell was going on, how could they turn me down when someone of Dickey's stature said I'm talented and worth their while?

Meanwhile my domestic life was becoming stranger by the minute, a surprise every step. Having shared the secret only with our parents prior to the event, Michelle and I eloped on a cliff in California (where we would relocate within a year's time), only to have some of our closest friends react angrily because we'd gotten married without including them. I wrote letter after letter after letter, apologizing for following our hearts and wedding ourselves without the big fuss everyone seemed to expect. Chris and I at least had made some notable progress as far as working past the wedge my good fortune had driven into our friendship, so his response to the whole thing was appropriately outrageous, just like the old days. He mailed me a one-page note, at the top of which he'd pasted a color picture of a scantily-clad brunette, lasciviously lounging in black panties and brassiere, and beneath which he'd typed, *See this? Take a good, hard look. Doesn't that* <u>*slaughter*</u> *you? Okay, now forget about it. Don't ever think of it again. Ever. Congratulations on the wedding.* Within a year's time, he and his girlfriend Chrisanne would tie their own knot.

Having smoothed-out as best we could whatever wrinkles remained amongst our friends, Michelle and I packed everything we owned into a big rented truck and drove 3,000 miles from both of our families before unloading it all into a three-bedroom house in Pasadena, California, one we were sharing with a great friend and former college roommate named Peter. Michelle was planning to enroll in a graduate program in clinical psychology, while I was to continue writing all those novels no one was reading, and the next sixteen months went by in a blur from which I would awaken as if from a nightmare into a very different world from the one I had known. Two-and-a-half months subsequent to our arrival in California (and two weeks before Christmas), a carbon monoxide leak in our house sent all three of us to the emergency room at four-thirty on a Saturday morning. Michelle and Peter were able to drive themselves, while I was strapped into a stretcher in the back of an ambulance with tubes shoved up my nose. Woozy and whirling like I was wasted on booze, I resented the paramedics who kept prodding me with ridiculous questions—'What's your favorite color? Where did you grow up?'—when all I wanted was to drift off and sleep. Those paramedics, I'd later learn, were saving my life—sleep might've meant the end of me. After five hours in an oxygen tent at Huntington Memorial Hospital, clear-headed and back on Earth, I was told that my intake of noxious monoxide was three times what Michelle and Peter had inhaled, yet I'd gotten out of the house just in time to secure a future for myself. I had a "28-count" of carbon monoxide poisoning, 40 being the magic number where brain damage begins with death soon to follow. 'You have a lot to be thankful for this Christmas,' a nurse said to me after all those hours breathing pure oxygen for the first (and last) time in my life. I was discharged late that afternoon and went home determined to believe her.

It wasn't easy, sad to say. Christmas came and went with just enough in the way of festivities to make Michelle and I both miserably homesick, and to make matters worse still we were fighting most of the time . . . with each other, with Peter, with our swinish landlord who arrogantly refused to pay my hospital bill even though it was *his* heater in *his* house that produced the life-threatening leak. Forced to fend for myself and hating that man for making me do so, I telephoned one lawyer and city official after another until he realized I was serious about suing, so finally coughed up the cash.

January brought my 27th birthday, which came and went with absolutely no festivities whatsoever—a situation that pained and disappointed me far more severely than I allowed anyone to see. Michelle and I spoke seriously of splitting up . . . years of stored resentments seeping to the surface . . . but in truth I didn't believe we would do it, not for a second, and Peter wisely remained on the periphery of it all by spending most of this time at his girlfriend's house. I plodded along with the still-unfinished third novel, but the mess of my life dragged at me every minute and made it virtually impossible to focus on fiction, especially since I'd wanted this particular book to have a happy ending. Fat chance. When the alarm horned at five for me to get up and get busy before the sun rose, I would shut it off and drift back to sleep, grateful for the opportunity to lose consciousness a little longer. It was sometime that same January that we got the news about Chris.

I have never written so much as a single sentence with any sort of map or outline to guide me, trusting instead the emotional truth of a story—as opposed to the factual one—to take the material in the direction it should go. There have been occasions, however, when I felt strongly that a particular story should end with a certain *feeling*, and I would lean my efforts toward getting it there even if I wasn't exactly sure how it was all going to play itself out. I passionately desired an affirmative *denouement* for my third novel, a book suffused with so much pain and loss and loneliness that it exhausted the reader by its conclusion and could have left him that way, but I loved the woman narrator and felt compelled to find some source of hope for her, some small scrap of something to hang on to after all she had been through.

But my god . . . Chris had cancer . . . thirty years old and he had cancer. He who turned around the life of a twelve-year-old; who was going to be the first to become famous, and who did everything against the odds like nearly failing out of high school but then going on to graduate from the most prestigious universities, BA from Yale and MFA from Columbia. What the hell was happening?

Less than a month later Michelle left for good, drove away in our car, crying, with all of her stuff crammed practically to the roof of it. February. I was in California, moved now into an efficiency apartment lacking even a telephone since I couldn't afford it, seventy degrees outside. Three months later Chris would be dead and I would be half-way to divorce. May. At six o'clock in the morning one day that dreadful month of May, I awoke from a fitful sleep to find my deceased friend standing at the foot of my bed.

'Don't hate me for dying,' he said.

'I don't hate you,' I answered aloud, 'I miss you.'

This is no joke. In fact, all these years later I am more convinced than ever that he was actually there . . . right there. The memory is very vivid. Maybe you're thinking I dreamed it, or imagined it, but he was standing in that room just as sure as I'm sitting here, writing this, telling you. What's the difference, anyway? Suddenly sobbing and scared to death I phoned a friend of mine that very minute and asked her to please come save me because I was terrified and alone with ghosts and when she got there ten minutes later I told her it was official—I had cracked.

At a memorial service held for him in Savannah, I saw my friend
for the very last time sitting on a table inside a small black box
no bigger than a square-foot, and after the ceremony some of us
who were closest to Chris—along with his parents—carried him
as he'd requested to the Ogeechee River outside of town where
we used to go canoeing once he had discovered Dickey. I was in
one of two boats and Chris sat on his crying widow's lap in the
other one. Once we'd located a suitable spot at which to spill him,
she opened up that black box to reveal something like a sandwich
bag inside, complete with a twist-tab, and within which was the
dirty proof of what it all comes down to.

I've taken up close to two pages with this but in truth it happened
a lot faster than that, relatively speaking—Lesson 3.

It wasn't until I moved back east some nine months later in an attempt to pull my life back together that I tried to reestablish contact with that other hero whose moves I once monitored almost as closely as my own, and by then I was looking at life from the standpoint of a survivor, just as Dickey had said of himself subsequent to the Second World War. I wrote Dickey a brief but all-inclusive letter that conveyed the whole of what I had been through without going into the minutiae of it, and awaited his response with an anxiousness I could do nothing to assuage. I finally finished that third novel, and even managed an ending that was optimistic enough to satisfy what I'd wanted for it, but months went by without a word, no response to my letter. I thought about starting a book that would deal—in a fictional format—with all that had happened in the past year, one that would either make or break me as a writer, especially now that I realized I was really on my own: without a best friend to share the solitary struggle; or a wife to love and encourage me; or an established artist to help push my work into print. I considered calling Coleman, but couldn't bring myself to do it—the last contact we'd had, he was himself suffocating under the rejections his own work was receiving, so I wasn't about to add to his woes. I still had that letter, at least, a framed page generously littered with descriptions like "dead serious" and "talented", and decided that regardless of how much or how little I accomplished in the public eye, I had that glowing recommendation hanging like a diploma to prove that there was a time when I had a brilliant future. My hero had said as much.

Those days were gone. Fact is, I had lost all faith in myself as a writer. Though the *person* had survived a year of dreadful misfortune, I harbored grave doubts about the writer, whose identity I must admit I was skeptical about even before Chris died . . . before I blew my marriage . . . before I fell out of favor with Dickey. Now that none of those people were around to lie to me, tell me I was worthwhile and could be a great writer if such is what I wanted, it seemed that some huge insurmountable obstacle had been placed in my ambitious path. How can a man overcome his own inherent mediocrity? I wondered.

He can't, I decided.

By virtue of being on the planet at the exact same misty moment in history as I was, Chris had challenged me to do just that. Without him here to goad me, however, the will would have either to rise to the occasion or capitulate to the obvious—it wasn't within me to do. It is a hell of a thing to have three novels written, a soul wrought on hundreds of pages that took many years' worth of joy and anguish and plain hard work to complete, yet still perceive yourself as incapable, a fraud. It isn't a question of quality, either: I could pick up any one of the three books and hold those hundreds of soul-weighted pages in my hand, and the question that would occur to me wasn't is this a great novel or is this a good novel, but is it a *novel*? Coming from such a perspective as that, how was I to start over, begin again with a brand new book to see if *this* time I might actually manage to write a novel—that indefinable, groped-after goal I had set for myself so long ago—especially when one considered the subjects I'd be forced to confront this time around?

One word: a book must always begin with one word . . . to be followed by another and then another until the writer has said what it is that is within his heart to say. So, searching deeply within myself, afraid and frustrated and alone, the word was finally found that would seem to be the *only* source for starting, the one place that could not be avoided forever and from which all feelings of success and failure would spring, regardless what the world said: *I.*

Once that simple word was written, I burned my way through the myriad feelings that had pained and scared and saved me over the past year by burying myself in that new novel only to see if I had the audacity to dig my way out, which took just over a year of my life. And my god what a ride it was—there were mornings when I wept writing those pages, mornings I laughed at them, scoffed at them, mornings I tore them up and threw them in the trash and swore I was done with writing forever. Then the next day I'd be right back in that seat, pen in hand, trying to find the next word like it might be the one to open the floodgates and lead to finishing the job. Which is exactly how it went, because one day I sat down to work and three hours later discovered it was done—when I surfaced and looked at what I had brought forth from that sad, regret-filled journey, I felt like someone with a new lease, a second chance. It was as if I had just finished my first novel, such was the sensation of having conquered something incredible. I was beginning to experience again at least some sense of personal satisfaction, something that had been missing from my life for far too many months, something vague and overwhelming that had nothing to do with professional ambition. In short, I was *alive*, and now I knew it. Chris had talked about dying with a regularity we sometimes made fun of—he wrote letters complaining of symptoms he was convinced were cancer while I wrote it off as a product of his supercharged sensibility. So, as with everything, he proved his seriousness by showing the way for the slow-witted. *Take nothing for granted*, the 14-year-old Chris had said to the 11-year-old me, standing stupefied after he'd shredded a piece of paper and restored it right before my very eyes. *Okay*, the 27-year-old me could say now, *I get it*.

Were that my 30-year-old friend was around to hear it.

Then something remarkable occurred: the novel Chris had submitted to fulfill his MFA requirement at Columbia, *The Dangerous Lives Of Altar Boys*, was picked up by a university press who thought enough of the novel to publish it despite the sorry fact that they would get no more work from its deceased author. I hadn't read the book, but Chrisanne decided to share the manuscript before its proposed release with some of us closest to Chris, so when the big brown package arrived in the mail I plunged right into it and read the whole thing in two days. In truth, I was disappointed when first I read it, because all I found in there were words typed onto sheets of bond paper. Chris was still dead and all the fun we'd imagined for our future had gone to the same long home that awaits all living things.

Which is to say I had expected much more than any book could ever hope to deliver. So I waited a week and started reading it again, only this time the scared lonesome beauty of the thing unfolded in front of me like nothing less than a miracle. Chris's presence rose up renascent out of those pages and sang me back home, reminded me how powerful was that very special energy he had, incandescent, and I laughed at its antics and cried at its sadness and finally decided for certain that my friend had indeed been sort of prophetic—he'd seen his own fate and faced it, wrote it right into his first novel. There were so many of us whose lives were impacted by Chris: his charisma could hardly be ignored even by those who were critical of him. So when two characters in his novel are discussing the premature death of their teenage friend—a boy blessed (cursed?) with a similar Chris-like charisma—and one says to the other, '*People like that die young. They have an influence on other people that lasts, but they don't . . .* ' it struck me that my friend had been well aware of what was expected of him, and had actually tried his best to acknowledge it, open his arms to Fate and say, 'I accept.' In the novel, Chris had skillfully divided his psyche into its two opposing duplicities—the go-getter who craves a life of action and consequence, versus the insecure play-it-safer who'd rather find his riskless comfort zone and stay curled up inside it like a cocoon. This time my reading proved that the book wasn't limited to words on a page at all—Chris was there, loud and clear and very much alive, like a friend you could call on the phone and say, *My god, your book was amazing . . .*

So when the favor was asked how could I refuse? Chrisanne wondered whether I would be willing to write to James Dickey about *Altar Boys*, ask him for an endorsement we could use on the dustjacket. She forwarded me the publisher's uncorrected page proofs of the novel to enclose with my request, so I sat down determined on a Monday morning to try to carve out what would end up being as difficult as anything I'd ever dared to write. As I perceived it, this was an attempt on my part to impose some sort of justice on the world, for Chris of all people rightly earned this endorsement (provided Dickey liked the book) and here was an opportunity for me to sacrifice my own selfish hopes and dreams and write to the man regarding someone other than myself. I felt completely confident that *Altar Boys* would win Dickey's favor, not only because the book concerned itself with some of the same issues to be found in his own endeavors, but also because, stylistically speaking, it was a meticulous piece of work in which all of the author's painstaking efforts could be seen by one with eyes for such a thing as literary risk-taking. *Chris was a great admirer of your work*, I wrote, *introduced me to it, in fact. And the notion of you reading his novel is one he surely would have seen not only as a triumph but as an honor. As it is I feel these things for him.*

The sad truth. I wept my way through the writing of that letter, spewed it out in a single emotional sitting and sent the package off that very afternoon, grateful to be finished with it. (Although I let myself linger a little over the publisher's page proofs, jealously marveling over the amount of money and attention they had devoted to my friend's book, and wondering if I would ever be allowed the luxury of seeing such done for me—forgetting for the selfish moment that such was a luxury even Chris would never enjoy.) The deadline for endorsements was bearing down on us, about which I had informed Dickey in the letter, so if he was going to contribute I knew we would hear from him within a few weeks' time.

We never did, and I decided then that, for whatever reason, he who had been so generous and good to me for so long had finally washed his hands of me. Who knew why? Who could speculate what might have been his motive for showing me nothing but silence after all of the interest he'd shown before? Perhaps he'd reread those early mediocre poems of mine, seen them for what they really were and decided—

A possibility I dared not admit to myself.

Dickey's third and final novel, *To The White Sea*, was actually in the bookstores for more than a few months before I even knew about it, but naturally the second I saw it there on the shelf I had to have it: despite our personal distance, Dickey was still an important artist, and I could never abide by a refusal to support his work over something so silly as his disregarding my pleas for attention (especially after all he'd done for me previously).

I'd read only about thirty pages before I threw in the towel, though, resigned to its inferiority: bored with the subject, peeved by the novel's arrogant and wholly unlikable narrator, and thoroughly displeased that Dickey had decided to enslave the style to first person when the result was as unpoetic as anything I'd ever read. He had turned his back on his strengths as a writer, I decided, and though that was his prerogative as the author it was mine to find a better book to read.

When *Altar Boys* hit the bookstores I bought two copies and proceeded to reread the published version, which sent my respect for the book soaring. Though it pains me to admit, seeing a published novel is a far cry from reading the same material in manuscript form, and tends to affect directly the way in which you see the book before you. Dean Rohrer's fittingly explosive cover-art, coupled with immaculate typesetting, thick pages invisibly bound, and complimentary blurbs covering the entire back of the book, caused me to see it now as a *novel*, whereas a manuscript seems more like the author's *attempt* at a novel. This is a hurdle every writer faces, and the fact that someone such as myself— who has spent so many years dealing with books in manuscript form—is guilty of this same misconception just goes to illustrate how very real and pervading a problem it is. Aside from the aesthetic differences in the packaging, I think the reason for this can be attached to our intuitive awareness of what a manuscript must go through in order to reach this final stage of the publishing process: that is to say, many people have read the book and deemed it worthy of a sizable investment of time and money and attention, so much so that they would spend months of their lives seeing it designed and laid-out and organized and type-set, finally printed and bound and covered to produce thousands of glossy copies that will then be distributed to hundreds of bookstores where it will be marketed and promoted as a work that should be read by the public at large . . . all of this quite in opposition to the thousands of awkward, bulky and difficult-to-deal-with documents comprised of loose, unbound pages that litter desks all over the world, of which nine such manuscripts I myself can claim to have contributed personally.

Reading the published version of my friend's book, I found myself highlighting with a florescent yellow marker damn-near every other paragraph, an old habit I'd acquired not from college classes, but from the budding novelist's desire to pay attention to the nuts and bolts of a book so as to learn something about the way words and paragraphs can be put together to produce a particular effect. I rarely look at the manuscript version of *Altar Boys* that I nevertheless treasure, and if I do it is only to appreciate Chris's homemade cover, a modified Bernie Wrightson image from the *Swamp Thing* comic; or his notation on the title-page that the novel was produced "entirely without computers"; as well as a desire to look at the few places where he made handwritten corrections in the margin—these things give me a concrete sense of Chris as having once been in my shoes, slaving over sentences he hoped would one day be read—and appreciated—by the world around him.

When reviews of the book began to appear I lapped them up thirstily as if it were my own work being discussed, and was thrilled to find that, for the most part, they were extremely favorable (our hometown newspaper in Savannah being, to this very day, the only periodical in the country to pan the book). There is no denying that I was enjoying vicariously what my own books had henceforth failed to provide me, but it was more than that. What seemed to matter most was sharing the loss of Chris, as one critic after another bemoaned the tragedy of such a singular talent being snuffed so soon, before he'd had the chance to do more. I was moved to tears more than once by some of the nice things said about my friend, particularly a review from the Philadelphia *Inquirer*, whose author obviously appreciated the subtle enormity of Chris's accomplishment: *This is the real thing*, he wrote, causing my heart to sink with sad gratitude, *writing done with everything on the line*. It was amazing to me that people who'd never met Chris could see so clearly what he was capable of, and the experience of witnessing this firsthand just reminded me why it is that I ever bothered putting pen to paper to begin with: done with a purity of purpose and a certain extreme measure of emotional sincerity, writing can cause a communion of souls who otherwise will never know of one another. In their own way, these people who so loved Chris's novel missed him every bit as much as I did, giving me a comforting sense of company in a time of unnamable sadness.

Eight years after the planned post-collegiate collaboration on film screenplays that never materialized, Lamar and I managed to make good on that long-ago commitment when we shared the task of adapting *The Dangerous Lives of Altar Boys* from a novel to a screenplay. This we did at Chrisanne's request, who fully realized that since a screenplay *would* be written no one was better qualified than the two of us, our lack of experience with the particular medium more than compensated-for by our closeness to Chris. The resulting script was long for a film screenplay (nearly 200 pages), but we had tried to remain completely true to our friend's book and keep intact some of its more idiosyncratic moments and flavors.

When we were told by those who "know best" that 75 pages needed to be trimmed from our script if ever it was to be considered a viable option, we bore down and did that too, though by the time it was done I had lost most of my fondness for the product, deciding that movies were becoming an increasingly shallow medium and very few people involved were interested in doing anything more than scratching the surface of things in a timely fashion—who had time anymore for subtlety and nuance or the long patient immersion into character? When, remarkably, actress Jodie Foster's film production company bought the rights for *Altar Boys* some time later, the first order of business was for them to hire a "real" screenwriter for the job. So Lamar and I patted one another on the back, reminded ourselves that we'd done the work for personal reasons having nothing to do with our ambition as writers, and tried not to think about the insane amount of money given the new guy for his version of Chris's story.

Mr. Dickey:

I'm thinking of you these days so decided to say it. In honesty it has been so long since last we spoke or corresponded that I am not even certain my name will mean anything at all to you, but that will not stop me from speaking those words I so often find myself feeling when my thoughts turn to you.

There was a time in my life, my youth, when you and your work represented all that was possible in a world that constantly confronts us with trouble, and like poor Job before us we grasp for something solid to cling to as Faith. For more years than I care to count that Something to which I clung has been the thought of you—all you've accomplished in your life and your work, all of the encouragement you were willing to share with someone young and already struggling against life's bleak anonymity—and for reasons unknowable to me I recently feel compelled to remind you of the fact.

Never cease to know, Mr. Dickey, that the world is a better place for your being in it.

As ever,

Michael Hanson

I believe the "unknowable reasons" may have been attributable to my recent reading of a poem called "Mangham," Dickey's amazing little masterpiece about a math teacher who suffers a stroke while lecturing a class but—pressing an ice-filled handkerchief to the side of his frozen face—goes on to complete the geometry proof he'd been working on the blackboard as if nothing in the world mattered more at that moment. I had sat awestruck some ten years prior while Dickey read this particular poem, and remember like it was yesterday the breathless exhilaration of both his rendering and my overwhelming response to it. Whenever I reread the poem, I always wonder whether it will produce the same sensations that coursed through the college undergraduate I was when first I heard it.

It did, on this occasion as on all others, which moved me to write to him. Honestly, I hadn't thought much about him since that time I'd tried, unsuccessfully, to read his latest novel, so what would end up being the fortuitous timing of the contact is as much a mystery to me as anything in this world. To my complete astonishment, an envelope bearing his old familiar letterhead appeared in my mailbox less than a week later, and despite our long stretch of silence I tore into it with all the same excitement hearing from him always elicited. The letter was frank regarding the severity of his physical condition, as for the past two years he'd been afflicted with jaundice (among other things). He did not speak then of the fibrosis of the lungs which was suffocating him, nor the chaotic state of his domestic life, the bitter divorce he was enduring as a 73-year-old. What he did was make it clear that my letter was helpful to him despite the scary mess that currently surrounded him. *When a sufferer receives a letter like yours—no, your letter—he is in the position of one hearing from a better universe: a place where kindness and generosity are natural to people, and are exercised without calculation. I am not given to gush, but I hope what I say here will register with you and that you will realize the depth of my response.*

It was this profession of gratitude, coupled with the same strange pull toward him I'd felt since first finding his work, that gave me the courage to contact him again to request a visit, and after two letters (plus a phone call) I was in the car headed to Columbia, South Carolina to see him, nervous and thrilled and, no denying it, *terrified.*

The drive took three-and-a-half hours, in which time I was able to listen in its entirety to an abridged reading of *Deliverance* on audio cassette, done by the man himself: I was psyching myself up, and it worked with a vengeance. An assistant to whom I'd spoken on the phone had given me directions to Dickey's house, so when I arrived in Columbia an hour ahead of schedule I made my way to a large depressing shopping center that I knew was within a few minutes of the place. I thought about finding someplace to get a drink, settle my nerves, then thought better of it, deciding I would rather the experience be raw and crystal clear. Even a cup of coffee was out of the question—I figured by the time I finished I'd be far too fidgety to sit still at all, frantic as I was already. Spotting what appeared to be a bookshop I headed straight to it and, walking in, discovered one of those huge cavernous stores you think will have virtually every book you could ever want to buy but in fact seems to have none of them.

Naturally I had to test the place by checking the Poetry section, but they didn't have him there so I went to Fiction and he wasn't there, either. Not believing it, I snagged the attention of a sales clerk and asked if they had any books by James Dickey, feeling foolish for the very asking. She said, 'Oh, yes,' so I decided she was going to lead me starry-eyed to a specific section devoted entirely to the local celebrity. Instead, she took me to a range of books under the heading SOUTHERN WRITING (evidence of our need to narrow everything into a category), where I did manage to locate one lone title by the celebrated National-Book-Award-winning author who lived less than ten minutes from this very store—a paperback of *Deliverance*, naturally. Dickey was indeed out of fashion, his literary stock frighteningly low, so much so that even his hometown stores apparently didn't bother to stock his books unless they happened to be best sellers.

I browsed around for roughly forty-five minutes, discovering that at least Dickey was in good company since this store had other notable shortcomings: only one title each by Faulkner, Fitzgerald, Steinbeck, and two by Hemingway (no Joyce at all). Such a lack of concern for literature by those purportedly there to serve it can be awfully discouraging if you take the time to notice, especially for those bent on joining the ranks of the aforementioned writers. I naively consoled myself that this was just a lousy bookstore, the exception rather than the rule. When I stepped outside again a mere fifteen minutes separated my mentor and me, just enough time to make a phone call to help bolster a suddenly-crumbling self-confidence.

My mom answered on the second ring, all excited to hear from me. I told her how nervous I was but she reminded me there really was no reason to be: I'd faced this before, albeit a decade prior, and this—in conjunction with all the correspondence we'd exchanged and the simple fact that Dickey had agreed to see me when clearly he could have avoided it—should reassure me, convince the skeptic there was nothing to fear. While what she was saying was true, it wasn't her words that would help relax me so much as the calming *sound* of her, along with the confidence she carried for me. Once we said our goodbyes and hung up,

I morbidly imagined the loneliness that awaited me when only the memory of my mom would be around to call on for occasions such as this one.

It was scorching hot, easily in the upper 90's, so despite the blasting AC my shirt was sticking to the seat as I maneuvered the car through the safe comforting streets of a typical middleclass suburb, the trimmed hedges and manicured lawns looking nothing like the stomping ground of one's literary idol, especially one with the wild-to-be-wreckage reputation of Dickey. Turning left onto Lelia's Court, I pulled into a driveway that appeared to be the place: a modest ranch-style house whose simplicity surprised me, such being the way our imaginations can get to conjuring when it comes to people we consider "famous". I sat still in the car for a few moments, drenched in anticipation and taking deep breaths of stifling summer air, then walked boldly to the door and rang that bell as if I actually belonged there.

A young man answered, catching me off guard, and led me to the living room where sat a stormy-haired shape surrounded by tall stacks of books. I was completely unprepared for his appearance: the powerful, barrel-chested man of my memory was now looking frail and very ill, his long arms leaned-out, his gaunt face pulled groundward by gravity, a wild head of thinning hair giving him a crazed look that seemed to me full of fear and angry intensity. Everything in sight suggested chaos, a life coming apart, as Dickey sat smack in the center of a room that was literally overflowing with books, not even shelved in bookcases, just stacked up on the floor in towers of ten all around him . . . there must have been hundreds of them taking up the better part of this big room in which a piano cowered in one corner. He held out his hand to me and said, 'You've had a terrible time, son,' referring to all of the despondent, self-absorbed letters I had sent to him unanswered while enduring divorce and the death of a best friend. And when I opened my mouth to respond what came out was, 'Haven't we all?'

My memory of all that was said during the three hours in that house is murky, I'm afraid—the part of the mind that could have held onto everything was undermined at the moment by a skeptical refusal to accept where I was and who I was with, even though there were times during the course of our visit when we were both silent, just sitting together without forcing conversation, and at those moments I distinctly recall reminding myself to take note of what was happening . . . that I was there . . . *right there* . . . and had better believe it because I wasn't going to be there for very long. Neither was he, which we both knew. (Anyone who saw him in his final months could not help but notice the ominous sense of closure that was enveloping Dickey, and he did nothing to try to conceal it.) Even now, as I sit here trying to reconstruct the reality of that room in which I sat with a man who marked my life forever, a hero who was dying, I have a hard time believing that I was actually there, *right there*, in the thick of it.

Periodically he was envictimed to a persistent hacking cough which would have its way with him for minutes at a stretch while I sat scared shitless, convinced I was witnessing the Last Gasp, his whole body broken up by it as he fought for air while a tube connected to a portable oxygen canister clung to his upper lip.

He twice mentioned his wife Deborah, who he was in the process of divorcing, but the anger in his telling persuaded me not to pursue the subject as it only appeared to infuriate him. He spoke of various writers, people like his friend Robert Penn Warren— men I saw as GIANTS—with a casualness I might slip into while mentioning my cat. (He told me that he and Penn Warren had filmed a documentary together, one in which they "interviewed" one another at their respective residences: Dickey traveling to Connecticut to converse at Warren's home, the latter then coming south to Columbia to talk to Dickey on his Lake Katherine dock, all of it apparently the brainchild of a public television producer. 'Next time you come down I'll drag it out for you,' he promised, sensing my enthusiasm.) He seemed pleased about the recently-published *Striking In*, (about which I knew nothing), a collection of some of his journals from the 1950's which also contained some poems—composed in the same long-past decade—that miraculously had never seen the light of publication. It must have been strangely satisfying for him to see such a personal thing published after forty years of writing, confirmation of a certain kind of literary success. When I asked how he thought those old poems in the collection held up, how did they strike him now, his reply had the perspective with which one becomes ever more familiar with the passing of years: 'I wish I could get that young man's angle on things again,' he said, not sadly.

What he was most excited about was a proposed film adaptation of his last fiction, *To The White Sea*, the only one of Dickey's books that I was completely ill-equipped to discuss since my false-start with the novel three years prior. Fortunately, he didn't get into specifics regarding the novel itself, sticking instead to prospective directors for the film, or actors he thought might be best suited to play his protagonist Muldrow. Though he had nothing directly to do with the project, he was very pleased about the interest others seemed to have in it, and ran through a long list of directors and actors to get my opinions on potential candidates. At the time, I was quietly depressed by this aspect of our visit, thinking that for Dickey to become absorbed by such a thing as a Hollywood adaptation of his work was beneath him. But I've revised my harsh judgment since then—for him it was part of the whole package, I think, yet another indicator that there was value in his work since so many others had an interest in it, not to mention the simple fact that Hollywood had—in at least one sense—*made* James Dickey (like it or not), certainly in the eyes of the general public who were, after all, the ones who paid for him the bills his true craft could never touch, providing more for his family than forty years of teaching and poetry-writing ever had or would. I'm sure that for Hollywood to make a big production from one of his books, particularly one published twenty years after *Deliverance* had made him a household name, would have done wonders for Dickey, and I'm speaking not only in the financial but also the spiritual sense.

Of course my friend Chris came up, the context being *Altar Boys*. Dickey did not mention the letter I had written him in that regard five long years prior, and seemed to have no knowledge of the novel having been published. This was somewhat shocking to me, having a hard time imagining that one's life could be so chaotic that he no longer even saw his own mail, but gave me a glimpse of just how out-of-control Dickey's world had come to be, confirmation of which would surface posthumously when biographers combed the specifics of his personal life for clues to his genius and mania. Dickey did admit that the name Fuhrman struck a familiar chord, so I said that was probably due to the fact that Chris had written to him while still an undergraduate at Yale.

Later, though, during a different conversation, he asked if I had mailed him photographs of me and some friends holding a blowgun-shot rattlesnake, acting on an essay he'd published—I swallowed hard, a great gulp of sad nostalgia and shortcoming that threatened to choke me up, and in a second's reflection was sorry for being there, as if I didn't deserve to be. 'That was Chris,' I said. 'He sent those pictures.' It felt like a confession.

At some point I told him how much I loved writing, how it gave me an excited sense of significance I could find nowhere else, but that I loathed the lonely anonymity of it. 'You'll have your time,' he said. 'Trust me.'

There were subjects I longed to broach but in the end lacked the bravery for doing so. I longed to ask how he felt about the fact that he was dying, was he afraid or at peace with it, and did he believe in any kind of physical or spiritual life beyond this one? (As if a careful reading of the poetry couldn't answer these questions.) Dickey is a man whose passion and intellect have inspired me in ways I can't begin to measure the depth of, thus an understanding of his feelings and beliefs as he faced this last great challenge, one I spend no little time obsessing over, could have proven invaluable to me. This was an opportunity of which I should take full advantage, I kept telling myself, for there are few people in the world with whom one could openly discuss the reality of death, and if anyone had the courage and the wherewithal to do so surely James Dickey did. *Just ask him*, I coaxed myself a thousand times that afternoon, but I never did, silently harboring a concern that to do so would only remind the dying man of that which he might wish to escape. At least for a little while.

Death did make an appearance, however, when I asked him if he was able to continue working despite his condition, to which he replied, 'A little. There are things I'd like to finish while I'm still here . . . still on this side of the shadow-line.'

Three hours later he remarked that he hoped I would do this again, pay him another visit, which I took as a not-so-subtle hint that it was time for me to be on my way. Having put it off until the very last moment, I pulled from the backpack I'd brought along a bound copy of one of my books that I wanted to give him, a novel thoroughly rejected by publishers but into whose female protagonist I poured every bit of my fear and joy and lonely longing, not to mention took a great many risks in the writing of: *Lissa* is a book I will always love even if the publishers couldn't care less. It was a good time to give him one of my novels, for I could do so now with a conscience clean of professional calculation: Dickey was no longer in any position to help get my work into print, so what motivated me was something else entirely. Simply put, handing him one of my manuscripts gave me as great a satisfaction as I have ever been fortunate enough to feel. He asked specifically had I signed it for him and I assured him I had, then he skimmed the manuscript only for a few moments (me mincing in my seat) before asking if I would do for him a favor. 'Take this and put it on my chair so I can have a good look at it, otherwise it's likely to get lost in the shuffle.' I knew what he meant, as the mountains of books stacked around him attested to the extent of the "shuffle." He instructed me as to where his study was located and off I went, navigating his household like it was an amazing museum. The hallway down which I traveled was a virtual tunnel of books shelved floor-to-ceiling on both sides, then taking a left I entered that sacred space I had seen described in innumerable articles and interviews: another library of books, only these were neatly arranged around the walls of the room. To either side of me were racked a variety of archery bows, some of them large and elaborate, the first evidence I had seen of the author as archer. And straight ahead of me was his "desk", stretching the entire width of the room before a rectangular picture-window which overlooked the lake on which he lived. I moved slowly to his seat and placed the manuscript in it, then remembered that risk leads to greatness (as Chris had written in *Altar Boys*). So I took a quick scan over both shoulders to insure that I was alone, and then did it: I picked up my manuscript and sat down in that seat, surveyed the view from that oft-dreamt vantage, and let the floodwaters roll over me.

Six years prior to that sainted moment I was still living in California, and, to satisfy a demand I had made of myself when first moving to the state, I took a pilgrimage to the enshrined home of another hero, the deeply-feeling and perhaps even prophetic poet Robinson Jeffers, whose "Advice To Pilgrims" I have carried in my wallet on a worn scrap of paper since my twenty-first year. One member of a guided group of seven, I made my sad excited way through Jeffers' uniquely primitive homeplace wishing only that I could spend a night there . . . feel for some short stretch of time the special energy that might remain embedded in the stones and wood of this home he had inhabited for the better part of fifty years. The last stop on the tour was Hawk Tower, his self-constructed stone monument to his wife Oona, and for me a symbol of the man himself that I had longingly looked at pictures of ever since I was a college student—in the base sat a large oak chair he had built and seated himself at in the mornings when he wrote. As our group exited the tower, the gracious guide (a middleaged man who knew I was a novelist and apparently noted the tears on my face when—earlier—he'd read to us some lines of Jeffers' verse) turned to me and, pointing to that special seat said, 'Why don't you just hang out here for a few minutes . . . see if you can get some inspiration.'

So down I went. The group moved on and for five full minutes I sat there, all alone in Jeffers's tower, riding the rollercoaster of sentiment that sent me reeling into mystical contemplation, convincing myself that I was *meant* to be there, sitting in that seat . . . that some strange communion of souls was in fact occurring which connected me in a very real sense to that man I so admired. There is no means to measure my gratitude for those few precious solitary minutes in that monument, and I feel absolutely no shame confessing that it actually felt *fated* . . . like an unlived moment that needed nothing more than *me* in order to become a real one.

So here we are again . . . climbing to the top of the first rise before the rollercoaster lets us loose to send us racing across Time like a track already laid down on which for us to travel. I gave no attention to the desk itself, what was on it, rather let my eyes wander out the window to take in the view, see some of what he saw when sitting there. The back yard was big and open before sloping down to meet the lake, and pushed up against some trees on the right-hand fringe was an upsidedown canoe that looked like it hadn't met water in a while. Ed Gentry, Dickey's *Deliverance* protagonist, lives on just such a property, overlooking just such a lake. I imagined the work being done from that seat . . . the things thought by a mind unlike any other man's . . . the powerful poems which had their humble beginnings right where I was sitting—what I'd give for just an hour of privacy to pen some kind of commemoration from that very special starting-place. I was overcome all-at-once by an inscrutable urge to cry, like something important was coming to a head and I wasn't ready, wasn't prepared, I needed more time. I couldn't have been in that seat for more than 10 or 20 seconds total (nervous as I was about "getting caught"), but already it seemed like days, years, like I'd been away on some extended spiritual journey and by the time I returned Dickey would say suspiciously, 'What took you so long?'

So I stood, placed on the now-vacant seat a manuscript in which an effusion of my emotional life was distilled, and walked out of that room full of confused feelings, the least of which wasn't the hope that I might actually summon the courage to ask if I could sit there at length . . . one of these days.

Our goodbye lacked drama, the finality of a last farewell. Why wouldn't it? I fully intended to make the trip to see him once more in a month or two, and Dickey had no cause to doubt that I would do so. I took his hand and told him to please take care, and he sternly admonished me to do likewise. 'Don't be so hard on yourself,' he said. I must admit that the only apprehensions I had about leaving occurred once I was out the door and in my car, sitting in the driveway staring at that simple suburban house where a great poet had just sacrificed three hours of his life for me. It may seem like nothing to some, but for one fighting for breath even as oxygen is being forced into both nostrils through a life-saving tube, the monumental sweep of Time must be slowed down to something small and seemingly insignificant—something like a moment.

The long drive home allowed me time to reflect over all of the things I had forgotten to ask him about—it occurred to me that, nervous as I had been, I should have compiled a sort of checklist beforehand. There were other people who had played a significant role in my development as a young writer, people with whom Dickey had had contact of one kind or another and about whom I would loved to have heard his opinion—people like filmmaker Sam Peckinpah who'd been considered to direct the movie version of *Deliverance*, or writer Frederick Exley who, according to biographers, actually phoned Dickey once to say he was committing suicide (he didn't). I also was curious to know whether anyone had approached him about writing his biography, something I had considered proposing while still a college student. The fact that I had forgotten to ask these things did not undermine me for long, however. Instead, I focused on the *next* visit, about which I could fool myself into thinking I'd be far more relaxed than on this one, thus could better focus on some of those things I wished to say. That very week, in fact, I dropped him a note just to reiterate my appreciation and assure him that I hoped to be back down his way sometime near the end of August, around five weeks later.

That Friday night when I arrived back from Columbia, I had drinks with three holy friends who wanted to hear all about my adventure visiting a hero, and I, having allowed Dickey's energy once again to infect me to the point of forgetting his physical condition, excitedly described my peak moments in his presence and vowed that I would see him again the following month. And wasn't this an amazing world that someone like me could see such a fantasy come to fruition? Sitting at a lovely bottle-glittering bar with favorite friends, I felt quite confident that the life we were then living was without a doubt one which many another only dreams of having: replete with fierce heartfelt gratitude, and harboring no regrets over what might be missing, none whatsoever.

I did not make it back that August, and six months later a friend phoned at seven o'clock on a Monday morning to tell me what I never wanted to hear. For years, literally, I had fantasized this, imagined what I would feel and—most importantly—what I might do to immortalize the moment somehow, make it different from all others. What I'd failed to realize is that this conjuring had always allowed me the luxury of Chris with whom to commiserate, the one who'd *found* the man for us and who was so adept at creating memorable moments. Yet Chris had been dead for five years, only I'd forgotten to remove him from the fantasy. So when the awful event finally came to pass, James Dickey wasn't the only one suddenly gone from the world.

Had someone shown me a map and pointed to that mountainous, youth-sprung place of peaks and possibilities where once my passions had soared, the location labeled by a best friend and named for a hero, I still could not now envision myself capable of reaching it, almost as if the vehicle needed to launch the journey no longer existed. The birds were singing outside the window and it was already sunny. I wanted to cry but couldn't for some reason—I simply sat frozen and stonefaced, wondering what on earth I was supposed to do with the information I'd just been given. We do die. *Harp on it*, Coleman once wrote, like a wiseman. You think you know this, are aware of it. You imagine what it will be like and even lose sleep over it sometimes. Then it happens to someone close and you realize what you really thought was there might be some way around it.

My initial pouting and despondency was purely selfish and harbored little consideration for those far closer to the man than I. I didn't think about Dickey's family—his two sons, Christopher and Kevin, or Bronwen, the 16-year-old daughter who'd have to adjust to a life lacking a father when the biggest concern for most of her peers would be getting a driver's license. Nor did I think about those friends who were closest to him, nor the readers all around the world who admired the man every bit as much as I did.

I thought about me. I thought about the sense of possibility Dickey had always embodied and wondered where now was I going to find it. I thought about the vain desire I'd secretly harbored for years to publish one of my novels before he died so he could see that his encouragement and support had not been for naught, that his belief in me was well-founded. I thought about the fact that the first hero I ever had was a pale, skinny 14-year-old named Chris Fuhrman, perpetually clad in corduroys and white t-shirt, who would years later introduce me to the work of poet/novelist James Dickey. These were the days when Chris convinced me there was nothing wrong with being ambitious, that the desire to make an impact on a par with Faulkner or Hemingway was nothing to be ashamed of or take lightly, and Dickey being in the world convinced us both that we didn't have to be dead in order to do so.

Or did we?

Three months later I picked up *To The White Sea* and tried again, this time determined to push my way through the thing come hell or high water. I'd been revisiting Dickey's poems from the 50's and 60's, and wanted simply to keep *feeling* him, even when I expected the work to be inferior to his earlier stuff.

After fifty pages I began to grow accustomed to the deliberate inarticulate style, and admired the author once again for his unflagging conviction toward doing something completely different each and every time he set pen to paper, even when it meant abandoning the poetic in exchange for an awkward voice that would more accurately convey the world as his protagonist Muldrow experiences it. I began then to enjoy the book, as unlikable as its narrator still seemed to me, and as I moved deeper into the narrative something curious began to occur: the more isolated Muldrow became the more interested I was in what he had to say. Furthermore, the farther he traveled physically, the more inward his journey began to appear, and this—coupled with an increasing personal efficiency that rose in direct proportion to his isolation, his solitude—caused me to see something emerging from the narrative that bore little resemblance to what I'd originally perceived as a guilty pleasure, an action/adventure story lacking any of the depth I'd always felt in Dickey's work.

Then: in the final fifteen pages Dickey did what I never imagined him capable of, not while speaking through this particular voice—he took my breath away. I read with something like awe overtaking me, gradually aware of an astonishment I never saw coming. Told in a butchered broken tongue that the poet of thirty years prior never would have employed, *To The White Sea* rose to heights in its conclusion that even I could not imagine for my favorite writer. Truth is, I had sold Dickey short, deciding that the man who produced works like the monumental "May Day Sermon" (what Chris and I used to call Dickey's *Ulysses*) was long gone, had squandered his strengths and pickled his talent in alcohol. Yet there I sat with the final page turned and tears on my face, all-at-once reminded of how the entire world can be reinvented with words on a page put precisely in place. Dickey's last book, different as it appears on the stylistic surface, falls right in line with the work he had been doing from the very beginning by concerning itself with one simple, profound notion: finding the center within oneself and operating outward from that source alone. And although such a pursuit would demand an individual's solitude, his isolation, if he was true to his own inner life he would willingly—even *gratefully*—accept the sacrifice it necessitated and realize that, ultimately, it connected him to the world in the purest, most essential sense.

The wisdom, of course, can be applied in whatever fashion one selects for himself, and if I doubted what I was doing writing those books of mine, if the will to keep at it was being called into question, it is par for the course that the answer came from that same hero who had sent me on the search so many years prior, and whose own example is in the service of the system of belief he so passionately espoused: that in the end we are all alone in this world, but there does exist a tacit spiritual connection that we should seek-out however we can. Words are one means to doing this, as inadequate as they seem at times. Spoken, they can bind us to all those sharing this space, this moment; written, they can connect us to that collective unconscious world of which we can hardly conceive during these noisy, device-distracted days of ours. This goes even for the lowly likes of a runt from Savannah, Georgia, who wanted his life somehow to matter more than it seemed to, and who *yearned* for acceptance, if not from without, at least—at last—from within.

Those I call heroes convinced me that *this* was the Way, the source of strength, and they wrote books to prove it. *Try to stay tough and sensible*, Chris wrote in the last letter I would ever receive from him, just three months before his death. *Life sure is hard . . . but there are still a few good things left*. Which is why I wept over the final pages of Dickey's last fiction, because within it I found one of those good things . . . the *feeling* . . . that oneness with the world which can only be realized within the confines of one's own heart. But then *shared* in some fashion . . . *any* fashion, in fact. So I clung to that book for many minutes after finishing, just gawking at it and turning it over in my hands and skimming its pages like it was this precious thing.

And it was *in my hands*, you see, the source of my tears: I was crying for the alienated yet self-redeemed Muldrow, whose spiritual transcendence might, after all, mirror our own. Which in turn caused me to cry for his creator, who at last had crossed that final chasm, as well. All of which led me to cry for myself, still struggling to find the vehicle, the voice: a means to reach a redhead riddled with fear and insecurity and doubt, afraid he'll amount to nothing. But therein lay the last lesson, my life, my love. A world opened with words, like a book. Wholeness and clarity . . . circle unbroken . . . *possibility* . . .

Dickeyland.